On the Road: Starting Out

Sheryl Garrett, CFP®
Series Editor

Adapted and compiled by
Ruth J. Mills

Dearborn™
Trade Publishing
A **Kaplan Professional** Company

President, Dearborn Publishing: Roy Lipner
Vice President and Publisher: Cynthia A. Zigmund
Senior Acquisitions Editor: Mary B. Good
Project Manager: Ellen Schneid Coleman
Cover Design: Design Solutions

© 2006 by Dearborn Financial Publishing, Inc.

Published by Dearborn Trade Publishing
A Kaplan Professional Company

A Stonesong Press Book

Project Manager: Ellen Schneid Coleman
Interior Design: Brad Walrod/High Text Graphics, Inc.

Printed in the United States of America

06 07 08   10 9 8 7 6 5 4 3 2 1

Library of Congress Cataloging-in-Publication Data
Starting out/edited by Sheryl Garrett; adapted and compiled by Ruth J. Mills.
    p.   cm.—(On the road)
    Includes index.
    ISBN 1-4195-0004-X (5 × 7.375 pbk.)
    1. Young adults—Finance, Personal.   2. Finance, Personal.
I. Garrett, Sheryl.   II. Mills, Ruth J.   III. On the road (Chicago, Ill.)
HG179.S8113 2005
332.024′01′0842—dc22   2005015088

Dearborn Trade books are available at special quantity discounts to use for sales promotions, employee premiums, or educational purposes. Please call our Special Sales Department to order or for more information at 800-621-9621, ext. 4444, e-mail trade@dearborn.com, or write to Dearborn Trade Publishing, 30 South Wacker Drive, Suite 2500, Chicago, IL 60606-7481.

Contents

Introduction

On the Road: Starting Out is the first in a new series of books from Dearborn Trade Publishing intended to help you deal with the financial issues, problems, and decisions concerning specific life events. The decisions you face when you're just starting out in life are obviously very different from the decisions you'll make decades from now when you're thinking about retirement. You also have different decisions and opportunities at this time in your life than a married couple with children has.

Because financial planning shouldn't be intimidating, we've created these books to take away the terror. On the Road books are like travel guides to help you make the best financial decisions at each stage of your life, in this case as you start out and begin your life as an adult. This book addresses the issues that concern you *now* and will help you to

- make a budget and live within your means
- establish credit and manage debt
- get the most money out of your company benefits plan
- rent an apartment or buy a house
- buy or lease a new or used car
- save, invest, and work with a financial planner
- get married (or move in) and make financial decisions with a partner

These financial decisions are part of your life's journey, so we've made them easy to navigate, with lots of helpful "Roadmaps" (charts and tables of financial information to help you with each issue or decision that comes up), "Tollbooths" that help you calculate your expenses or savings, and "Hazard Signs" that caution you about some money pitfalls to watch out for. We've also included a section called "What to Pack," so you'll know the forms and other information you need to get a mortgage, for example. We've made sure you'll know what we're talking about, by providing "Learn the Language" definitions of unfamiliar or technical terms particular to each financial topic. And we've included "Postcards" that tell helpful stories of how other people have made successful financial journeys.

Finally, the end of the book includes an "Itinerary" or recap that reviews the key actions you should take at this point in your life, all of which are discussed in detail in the seven chapters of this book. The end of the book also includes a list of other books to turn to if you want more in-depth information on buying a home or a car or on budgeting, saving, investing, and financial planning for college, retirement, and other goals.

We hope you find this "travel" guide helpful as you map your route to financial success and peace of mind. Life is an adventure, and money paves the way. So let's get started on the road. The light is green, put your pedal to the metal, and go!

Plan Your Trip

Creating a Budget

▶ Where Are You Now?

So you're thinking about moving into your own place: congratulations! Maybe you've already done it. If so, it's even more important that you read this book to help you organize your financial life. Living on your own is a big step, but almost everyone has to do it sometime. You just want to make sure you have the financial wherewithal to do so. Can you afford your own place? After all, you don't want to have to move back in with your parents once you've left the family nest, right?

The fact is that more and more of us do live with our parents, so there's no shame in doing that until you're certain you can make it on your own. According to the U.S. Census data for 2002, about 14 percent of men and 8 percent of women ages 25–34 live with their parents. That's more than twice as many men and women who lived with their parents in 1960, when people often married at younger ages and moved out of the family home earlier. Another factor contributing to the increase is the fact that it is a good deal more expensive to live on your own today than it was back then.

It's a big step, so before starting out on the road to independence, you should know whether you have enough money to pay your rent and other bills. The first thing you should do to prepare to live on your own is create a budget.

Roadmap 1.1 will help you get started: Use the simple form provided to list all your assets. Some items may not apply to you; for example, if you're just starting out, you probably don't own any real estate yet. You may also have limited investments, if any at all, so you may not need to worry about those. Still, the list is a good way to start thinking about what you do have, as well as what you might have someday.

What Are the Speed Bumps?

Now that you know the amount of your assets, you need to figure out what you owe and what you're spending. Then you need to estimate what your new life is going to cost. So first, make another list of everything you currently owe to everyone. Don't panic: You just need to know the grand total, to compare it with your total assets. This calculation will not only determine your current net worth, but it will also help you determine whether this is the right time to go off on your own, and if so, the type of housing you'll be able to afford. Of course, in addition to your total assets, you should factor in your income, which isn't listed as an asset item on Roadmap 1.1 because it's ongoing.

Roadmap 1.2 lists all the big expenses we could think of that you might need to pay for. Again, many of these, such as alimony, child support, mortgages, and back taxes, probably don't apply to you. But you might have credit card debt, medical expenses, student loans, and car loans to pay off. List everything that applies to you, so you'll have a clear picture of where your money is currently going. Then subtract your total liabilities from your total assets to find out your total net worth. It's a good idea to do this task and update your financial information once a year so you know where you stand. Many people do this right after the New Year (as part of their New Year's resolutions); others do it during tax season, right before or after April 15.

It's now time to make a list of all your regular bills: your rent (or mortgage, if you've already bought a home), utilities (electric, gas), phone bills (including your cell phone), groceries, car payments and insurance, credit card payments, and student loan payments. Roadmap 1.3 can help you get

Roadmap 1.1

Your Assets

Assets—What You Own	Amount
Cash on Hand	_____
Checking Accounts	_____
Savings Accounts	_____
Money Markets	_____
Other	_____
Personal Property: (Present Value)	
Automobiles, Vehicles	_____
Recreational Vehicle/Boat	_____
Electronic Equipment	_____
Home Furnishings	_____
Home Entertainment Equipment	_____
Appliances and Furniture	_____
Collectibles/Antiques	_____
Jewelry	_____
Other	_____
Investments: (Market Value)	
Cash Value Life Insurance	_____
Certificates of Deposit	_____
U.S. Treasury Bills and Savings Bonds	_____
Stocks	_____
Bonds	_____
Mutual Funds	_____
Limited Partnerships	_____
Annuities	_____
IRAs—Regular/Roth/Keogh Plan	_____
401(k), 403(b), or 457 Plans	_____
Pension Plan/Retirement Plans	_____
Other	_____
Real Estate/Property	
Principal Residence	_____
Second Residence	_____
Land	_____
Income Property	_____
Other	_____
Personal Loans Receivable (money that other people owe you)	_____
Total Assets	_____

Roadmap 1.2

Your Expenses and Debts

Liabilities—What You Owe	Amount
Current Debts:	
Credit Cards	_____
Department Store Credit Cards	_____
Medical bills	_____
Back Taxes	_____
Legal bills	_____
Alimony	_____
Child Support	_____
Other	_____
Loans	
Education/Student	_____
Automobiles, Vehicles	_____
Personal (from family or friends)	_____
Home Equity	_____
Bank/Finance Company	_____
Recreational Vehicle/Boat	_____
Life Insurance	_____
Retirement Accounts	_____
Other	_____
Mortgages	
Principal Residence	_____
Second Residence	_____
Land	_____
Income Property	_____
Other	_____
Total Liabilities	_____
Total Assets	_____
− Total Liabilities	(_____)
Total Net Worth	_____

Roadmap 1.3

Your Monthly, Regular Bills

Expense	Amount
Rent (or monthly mortgage payment)	_____
Utilities (gas/electric)	_____
Groceries	_____
Car Payment	_____
Car Insurance	_____
Commuting expenses	_____
Health insurance	_____
Medical expenses and prescriptions	_____
Cable or Satellite TV	_____
Student loan payment	_____
Credit card payment	_____
Second credit card payment	_____
Third credit card payment	_____
Local phone	_____
Long-distance phone	_____
Cell phone	_____
Other	_____
Total	_____

started. If you haven't yet rented an apartment or bought a home, you'll be estimating some of these expenses.

Some of the things on this list may overlap with items on your list of total liabilities, but as much as possible, try to keep Roadmaps 1.2 and 1.3 separate. Roadmap 1.3 should be your monthly expenditures, to show what your minimum monthly costs are, and whether you can afford more, based on the salary you're currently earning. These unavoidable expenditures need to be paid before you can even think about any discretionary spending, so let's get them out of the way.

What Are Your Regular Pit Stops?

Of course, just driving back and forth to work is no fun: You need to take some road trips, too, for balance! So think about all the things you buy regularly that you think you can't live without. Are you spending lots of money in bookstores? At magazine kiosks or newspaper stands? At your local music store? The local pub or corner coffee shop? On dates, nightlife, or clothes? At the movies or the video store?

Roadmap 1.4 should help you think about these out-of-pocket expenses that are so easy to forget about because you're not paying them by check every month. But just because they're paid from cash on hand doesn't mean you'll always have plenty of it! So get to know where your money is going. Try to estimate what you're spending monthly on each of these expenses, and if you can't do that now, write down everything you spend for a month and use that as an estimate for the whole year. Include all the things you buy regularly, like magazines (either by subscription or individual copies), the daily and Sunday newspapers, your morning coffee, lunches at work, and all the money you spend on going out with friends or dates.

Be as specific as you can in recording the costs of items because you'd be surprised how all these little expenditures can quickly add up to a lot. If you don't know where your money is going, you can't do anything to reallocate it to what you really want to buy or save. So start making your list and be honest with yourself! This process may sound tedious, but many people are absolutely astounded when they find out what they spend in a month on drinks with friends, for example (all those $5.00 beers) or on cappuccinos! Then if you decide to cut back in one or more areas, you'll be doing it consciously, in order to save money for something else.

How to Stay on the Straight and Narrow Road

Now that you know where you're spending all your money, think about whether that's really where you want it to go. For instance, do you really need to buy a café latté everyday? Are you reading all the magazines you buy at the newsstand or that you subscribe to? Are you actually going to the gym you joined, after paying for the annual membership? Do you need to have every new CD that comes out, or could you be more selective in what you buy? And if you're going out every weekend night (or more), think about ways to economize: Find two-for-one happy hours (preferably that serve snacks so you won't have to spend as much on dinner), hang out at nightspots

Roadmap 1.4

Your Walking-Around Expenses

Expenses	Amount
Books	_____
Magazines	_____
Newspapers	_____
CDs	_____
DVDs	_____
Coffee/Sodas/Juice Drinks Bought on the Go	_____
Cigarettes	_____
Lunches out	_____
Dinners with Friends	_____
Dates	_____
Movies/Clubs/Bars/Nightlife	_____
Sports Events/Team Memberships	_____
Memberships/Dues (other organizations)	_____
Clothing/Shoes	_____
Laundry/Dry Cleaning	_____
Hairdresser/Barber	_____
Manicurist/Tanning salon	_____
Vacations/Weekends away	_____
Summer Share	_____

Savings*

Regular Contributions to 401(k)	_____
Regular Contributions to Savings Account	_____

Total

	_____

*Savings is listed as a walking-around expense because these contributions are changeable. You can increase them when you're ahead of the game and decrease or eliminate them if you find you need that money to pay off bills or loans. Then, when you're back on your feet, you can increase the contributions again, just as you might increase other expenditures when you're flush.

that don't have a cover charge, or eat dinner at home before going out with friends so you won't have to pay for an expensive dinner in addition to the festivities that follow.

Here are some other rules of the road for living on a budget:

Set aside all the money you need for regular bills before spending a dime on anything else. Try paying your bills as soon as they come in (even if they're not due for a couple of weeks) so that you won't forget about them and incur unwanted late fees and finance charges. You'll also know sooner each month how much money you have left over to save or spend.

Buy in bulk, whenever you can. You might have made fun of your mother for always buying the jumbo size peanut butter and the 12-roll package of toilet paper, but if you have room, buying in bulk is much more economical. Purchasing necessities from the supermarket or drugstore also costs much less than running to the all-night deli, where you'll pay a relative fortune. Why do you think they call them "convenience" stores?

Pay cash for everything until you know how much money you have. This is the best way to know if you can afford something: If you can't pay for it in cash, you shouldn't be buying it. This means you need to save up for all of your big purchases, whether it's a leather jacket or a bunch of CDs. At least you'll have the peace of mind that you're not going to get a killer credit card bill at the end of the month, just when the rent and all your other bills are due. Cash is the only way to pay unless you're tracking all your credit card expenditures as you make them, which some people do. Chapter 2 discusses credit in much more detail, but in the meantime, Roadmap 1.5 shows a simple way that you can keep track of your expenditures. Record the following information for each credit card you own: It's as easy as one, two, three.

1. Find out when your credit card closes its billing cycle, for example, on the 26th of the month.
2. Record the amount of each purchase made during your billing cycle. If you buy something during a calendar month but after the end of the card's billing cycle (for example, you buy an item at the end of January, but you won't be billed until February), enter the amount of that purchase in the next month's column; it will appear in next month's billing cycle.
3. Jot down the date and a one-word description of your purchase.

Keep track of your expenses. In addition to tracking your credit card purchases, you might also consider keeping track of all your expenditures. This strategy is especially helpful if you find yourself having trouble staying on the straight and narrow road and living within your means. Roadmap 1.6 is a yearly budget worksheet that helps you get a clear view of the road ahead. It will also tell you when you'll need to spend money for particular expenses, such as holidays, vacations and other trips, and birthday, wedding, graduation, and other gifts. Roadmap 1.7 shows you what the budget worksheet might look like after it's filled out, though each person's will be different, of course. Roadmap 1.8 then breaks the yearly budget down into monthly amounts, using the information you listed in Roadmap 1.3. You should fill out one of the worksheets in Roadmap 1.8 every month, so you can track whether you're coming up short or coming out ahead at the end of each month.

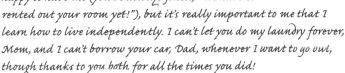

Dear Mom and Dad,

I found an apartment! I guess you've realized I didn't really want to move back home after graduation. I know you both would have been happy to have me (you've always joked, "We haven't rented out your room yet!"), but it's really important to me that I learn how to live independently. I can't let you do my laundry forever, Mom, and I can't borrow your car, Dad, whenever I want to go out, though thanks to you both for all the times you did!

Luckily, two of my college friends also wanted to stay here and find jobs. Of course, our new starting salaries didn't leave much for rent money unless we pooled it. So after pounding the pavement and calling everyone who might know of something affordable, we found a two-bedroom apartment with a living room large enough for a futon sofabed, and we divvied the rent according to room size. I'm taking the living room because it's bright and sunny, and after sharing a room all those years with my sisters, I won't mind my roommates marching through it to get to their rooms!

Wish me luck with the move! I'll call soon.

Roadmap 1.5

Credit Card Purchase Record

JAN		FEB		MAR		APR		MAY		JUN	
Billing Cycle Closing Date:											
Purchase	Amount	Purchase	Amount	Purchase	Amount	Purchase	Amount	Purchase	Amount	Purchase	Amount
3/gas	14.91										
7/shoes	20.82										

Credit Card Purchase Record

JUL		AUG		SEP		OCT		NOV		DEC	
Billing Cycle Closing Date: ___		___		___		___		___		___	
Purchase	Amount	Purchase	Amount	Purchase	Amount	Purchase	Amount	Purchase	Amount	Purchase	Amount

Yearly Budget Worksheet

Year 20____

(Non-Monthly Anticipated Expenses)

FIXED AND ESTIMATED NON-MONTHLY EXPENSES

		JAN	FEB	MAR	APR	MAY	JUNE	JULY	AUG	SEPT	OCT	NOV	DEC	TOTAL	MO. AVG.
Housing	Property Tax/ Homeowners Insurance														
	Home/Yard Maintenance														
	Utilities														
Transportation	Auto Insurance														
	Auto Expenses														
Health	Insurance— Other														
	Medical Expenses														
	Dental/Vision Expenses														

Additional Non-Monthly Expenses

Dues/Fees	
Education/Tuition	
Clothing	
Recreation	
Vacation/Trips	
Gifts—Birthday	
Gifts—Other	
Holiday Events	
Children's Activities	
Pets	
Total	

Reserve Savings:　　Total Expenses $ _____ ÷ 12 = $ _____ /Month

Roadmap 1.7

Yearly Budget Worksheet–Sample of Possible Expenses

(Non-Monthly Anticipated Expenses)

FIXED AND ESTIMATED NON-MONTHLY EXPENSES

		JAN	FEB	MAR	APR	MAY	JUNE	JULY	AUG	SEPT	OCT	NOV	DEC	TOTAL	MO. AVG.
Housing	Property Tax/Homeowners Insurance														
	Home/Yard Maintenance			Door 250	Yard 150			Drapes 250						650	54
	Utilities *Sewer*			65			20			50			85	220	18
Transportation	Auto Insurance	*Van* *Car*								500 / 425				1,000 / 850	154
	Auto Expenses		Lube 25	Tires 250		Lube 25			Lube 25	Lic. 100	Lic. 80	Tune-up 150		655	55
Health	Insurance—Other *Life*		80			80			80			80		320	27
	Medical Expenses	Rx 75		250		Dr. A 20			Rx 75			Lab 70		490	41
	Dental/Vision Expenses		Dental 750				Vis. 300		Dental 75					1,125	94

The following is a non-monthly expense budget worksheet.

Category													Total	÷12 /Month
Dues/Fees /Taxes	Prof. Lic. 95		Tax Prep 300		Ent. Bk 35	AAA 35	License 130			Gym 55			650	54
Education/Student Loan · Tuition		Seminar 150					85	Seminar 100		85		85	590	49
Clothing - Child Shoes/Coat 320			350		800		400	Season Ticket 75					1,070	89
Recreation Concert 60			Fish Lic. 35										170	14
Vacation/Trips	Ski 250									300			1,350	112
Magazines	YM 16		Kip 20									BL 39	75	6
Gifts—Birthday 25	15	50			15	100		100		75			380	32
Gifts—Other Anniv. 40		WWF 25	Grad. M. Day 60 / 50	F. Day 30		G.P. 30	Shower 35	Wedding 40				Xmas 700	955	80
Holiday Events			Easter 25			40	Halloween 60		TG 70			Xmas 400	595	50
Children's Activities 65			Field Trip 100		Camp 150	Lessons 65		School Photos 75 / 50					505	42
Pets														
Donations 15		WWF 25				G.P. 30		RC 50				CRS 100	220	18
Personal Perm 80			25			Perm 80		25					210	18
Total	680	1,316	1,965	600	725	1,350	600	905	1,225	505	885	1,324	12,080	1,007

Additional Non-Monthly Expenses

Total Expenses $ 12,080   ÷ 12 = $ 1,006.67 /Month

Reserve Savings: _____

Rounded Up 12,080

Roadmap 1.8

Monthly Budget Worksheet

INCOME SOURCE:

Net Income Total Amount:

Expenses	Amount	Date Due	Date Paid	Date Rcv.:					
Mortgage/Rent									
Car Payments									
Other Loans									
Internet Access									
Insurance									
Clubs/Dues									
Savings									
Electricity									
Oil/Gas									
Water/Garbage									
Telephone/Cell Phone									
Cable TV/Satellite									

Fixed Amounts

Fixed Variable

Category	Subcategory									
Fixed Variable	Groceries									
	Meals Out									
	Auto Expense/Gas									
	Church/Charity									
Occasional	Household									
	Personal									
	Clothes									
	Medical									
	Child Expense									
	Recreation									
	Miscellaneous/Mad Money									
Installment	Credit Cards									
Total	Total Income									
	Total Expense									
	Total Excess									
	Total Short									

Roadmap 1.9

Goals Worksheet–Immediate/Short-range Goals

Priority	Goal	Target Date	Cost Estimate	Amount Already Saved	How to Achieve (Amount per month, second job, etc.)

Goals Worksheet—Middle- and Long-range Goals

Priority	Goal	Target Date	Cost Estimate	Amount Already Saved	How to Achieve (Amount per month, second job, etc.)

Where Do You *Really* Want to Go?

Finally, what's not on any of your lists so far? What do you wish you could buy that you currently can't afford? Roadmap 1.9 is a simple goals worksheet that you can use to list all your financial goals, both short- and long-term. For example, you might want to buy a new computer, a new stereo system, a wide-screen TV, or a new car. Or you might want to buy new furniture, frame some artwork for your new home, or splurge on new clothes. Or maybe you want to travel, which can be a significant expense.

You might have longer-term goals. Perhaps you're saving to go back to school to get a master's degree, or maybe you want to sock away money for a rainy day. Maybe you want to retire while you're young, and you're eager to start saving and investing aggressively so you can do that. Or perhaps you want to save up to buy a house so you can stop paying rent. Roadmap 1.9 can help you because it requires you to consider the time frame and the cost for what you want to achieve, which is the first step to realizing your goals.

Watch Out for Tolls

Establishing Credit and Managing Debt

Now that you have a budget and a better idea of what your expenses are, you should establish some credit, which can help you meet your financial goals down the road. You also need to know something about managing debt so that it doesn't manage you!

Many of us get into financial problems because we lack an education about how the credit system works. Few schools teach this topic, and most parents don't teach their children how to handle credit and manage money. Unfortunately, people often learn about credit and finances the hard way: by getting into debt, which creates negative entries that can remain on their credit reports for up to 10 years. To help make sure that doesn't happen to you, this chapter will put you in the driver's seat.

▶ Check Your Mirrors and Adjust Your Seat: Why Good Credit Is Important

Having one or more credit cards is critical to being financially independent because many purchases can only be made with a credit card or a debit card. And although paying cash for everything is a good habit, paying only with cash will not help you establish credit because you will have no record of your payment history. In today's society, you can't really function without establishing credit: Without credit, you can't buy a home or car unless you can pay for it entirely in cash. And without a major credit card, you can't rent a car, reserve a hotel room, or buy airline tickets. In other words, you're stalled and out of gas.

You can have credit, however, without having debt by paying off your credit card balances in full when your statements come due. This habit is a good practice, and it shows up on your credit report as payments made on time. As a result, you establish a positive payment history that can be beneficial when you try to qualify for a mortgage.

In addition, you should have at least one or two credit cards in your own name. It's not enough for you to be an authorized user of someone else's credit, such as your parents or some other family member. Although it may help you in the short run, it won't in the long run because you need to establish credit for yourself.

The same is true if you are married and are using your spouse's credit card. If the credit card is only in your spouse's name and then you get divorced, you won't have an established credit history. Your credit report may show "no record found," which can be interpreted as having bad credit. Again, because the credit cards are in another person's name, you are only a user of the card. Sometimes the credit card company will state this fact on your credit report, but don't count on it. By the way, being an authorized user of someone else's card is not the same as having a *joint* credit card, where the card is in your name as well as someone else's. Obtain your credit report from all three of the credit reporting agencies: Experian (formerly TRW), Trans Union, and Equifax (discussed later in this chapter). Then check the reports to find out if any of the accounts you are using are listed there.

For New Drivers: Getting Your First Credit Card

Obtaining your first credit card is often a Catch-22 situation: You can't get a credit card until you've established that you are creditworthy, and you can't become creditworthy until you have a credit card in your own name. Fortunately, the major credit card companies (Visa, MasterCard, American Express) offer credit cards to college students and recent grads. They buy mailing lists of graduating seniors, who then find their mailboxes stuffed with credit card offers. But if you didn't go to college (only 27 percent of

Americans have a bachelor's degree), you'll have to find another way to get the attention of credit card companies.

Getting Your Driver's License: How to Qualify for Credit

Qualifying for credit is an art. You need to know what you are getting yourself into before you complete any credit application. You need to know what the credit grantor is looking for in order to get an approval. And you need to know what type of credit and terms you are applying for. Too often, individuals are shocked when they are issued credit, and they discover the terms are different from what they thought they would be.

Before applying for any line of credit, stop and do your homework. Read the fine print on the application. The differences in interest rates, fees on cash advances, annual fees, late fees, and payment requirements can be vast. For example, interest rates can be calculated in different ways:

► on a daily basis, in which interest charges start accumulating when a purchase or charge is made, or

► on a prorated basis, in which no interest is charged until a balance remains in a new billing cycle, which usually includes a 25-day grace period.

To decide whether to approve your application, a credit grantor will review your credit history (if you have any), the length of your employment, whether you own or rent your home, if you have a checking and savings account, and your credit rating. Using the information you give on your credit application, the credit grantor will assign a certain number of points to each category that will add up to give you a credit score. If the score is high enough, and your credit report is satisfactory, your application will be approved. Congrats! You have a green light, so get ready to hit the highway.

When you are trying to establish credit, credit grantors are looking for six months to two years of credit and payment history. Each company has its own criteria for determining to whom they should give credit. In general, a potential creditor is looking for the "three Cs" of credit:

1. *Capacity.* The capacity to pay is determined by your employment as well as by the length of time you have been employed. (More on employment in the next section.) Capacity also includes your expenses and the number of dependents you have (if any). Creditors then determine how much you can afford to borrow or how high to set your credit limit.

2. ***Character.*** The credit grantor evaluates your character by reviewing your credit history and paying habits. This information is obtained from the Experian, Trans Union, and Equifax credit reports.

3. ***Collateral.*** When a credit grantor is reviewing your collateral, it wants to see what assets you have other than your income, such as a savings account, investments, and any property you own.

Creditors want to know your employment history. Creditors want to know about your income, bonuses, and any commissions you have received. Most credit grantors want to see that you're driving safely and at a steady speed: They're looking for at least two years of employment at your current job. If you've been at your present job less than two years, you'll need to supply your employer's name, your position or title, your line of work, and the dates of your current and previous employment. If you had a lapse of time between jobs, you're out of gas. The credit grantor may not approve your credit application.

Another thing a credit grantor is looking for is the number of years you have been employed in your current line of work. If you've changed your occupation and have worked in your new field less than two years, you may not be approved. Hopefully, this will not be another red light on your journey.

Creditors are wary of solo travelers. If you're self-employed, you'll probably have greater difficulty getting credit than those who work for someone else because your income is harder to verify. You're also perceived as a greater credit risk because your income flow is not consistent. Many people who are self-employed have a poor credit history because their income is not stable. Finally, most self-employed people write off numerous expenses on their tax returns, which offset their incomes. You may have a steady cash flow, but a creditor reviewing your 1040 federal tax return may think the income appears low due to your write-offs on Schedule C of your IRS form.

Therefore, to get credit approval, you must be self-employed at least two full years. Again, creditors are looking for reliable drivers. Make a photocopy of any 1099 forms (reports of freelance income) that you receive from employers and attach them to your application. If you have contracted with any specific companies to do work for a certain length of time, list the company on the application and the income you are receiving.

If your company is incorporated, make sure the income you are receiving can be verified with your pay stub or yearly W-2 forms. If you're the majority owner, they'll want tax returns. Again, before applying for any credit, find out what the lending institution is looking for before you send in your application. If you can provide the required documents, don't hesitate to apply. If you fall short, gather the necessary information before you reapply.

Creditors consider whether you own or rent your home. A credit card company will look more favorably at your application if you own your home, but this obviously isn't the case for most people just starting out on the road to financial stability! If you rent, the company will look at how long you have lived at your current residence. If you move frequently, your application will be denied. In general, a creditor will look at your past two years of residency, though some creditors may look as far back as five years. If the credit grantor feels you are stable, regardless of whether you rent or own your home, your application will be approved. If you're not out on your own yet, you'll need to rely on some of the other ways described in this chapter to get credit. You'll need to show that you're stable and financially solvent via your bank accounts. To help you attain this goal, try to make deposits on a regular basis, and don't bounce checks. To prove stablity regarding your employment, try not to job hop too much until you've established some credit.

If you're applying for a mortgage rather than a credit card, a lender will look at your credit history and how long you have lived at your present address. The creditor will verify your length of residence by contacting your landlord or mortgage lender. Whether you pay your rent or mortgage on time is reviewed closely because it may indicate how you will pay your new loan.

Even if you are only trying to rent a home or an apartment, a credit report may be requested. A credit report tells a complete story of your paying habits, how much you owe, if you are overextended on your accounts, and what your balances are. It also reveals your current address, previous address, and occasionally your employer.

Creditors look at your checking and savings accounts. Creditors want the security of knowing that you have money in a bank account, especially because you need to make payments with a check or a direct withdrawal system. You don't necessarily need to have both a checking and savings account. However, you receive a higher credit score if you have both. Be sure to list the name, address, and account numbers on the credit application whenever asked. Specify which account is your checking and which is your savings account.

Creditors assess your stability. Overall, the more stable you appear, the better the chances of an approval on your credit application. The credit grantor wants to feel secure that if you do not make your payments, it has a means of collecting the debt. Most credit cards are unsecured, meaning that the money loaned is not guaranteed by an asset. A mortgage is secured by a house or property; a car loan by the car. In each case the lender can repossess the asset—the house or car—if payments are not made. In some states, a creditor's only recourse to collect a debt is to get a judgment made against you in court, and then obtain the payment from you when you sell or refinance your home or other property. Obviously, if you don't own property, the credit card company has even less recourse.

How Your Credit Is Scored

If a credit grantor subscribes to each of the credit reporting agencies, it can have access to a special credit scoring system that the credit reporting agencies use to analyze your credit reports. This system is known as the FICO score, which is an acronym based on the name of the company that developed it, Fair Isaac Corporation. A score can range from zero to 900 points. Using a combination of factors, including your credit payment history, outstanding credit, credit history, pursuit of new credit, and types of credit, the FICO score will reveal if you are deemed creditworthy.

For example, suppose you're in the market for a new car. The car dealer would request a copy of your credit report from a credit reporting agency. It will reveal your paying habits and FICO score. If you have a FICO score of 700 points, you would be automatically approved for your car loan without having to supply any further documentation. If your FICO score falls below 700 points, the dealer may require more documentation from you to get the loan approved.

Whether you're pursuing a car loan, mortgage, or credit card, each lender has its own criteria in determining what FICO score you should have. In addition to the FICO score, if there is any negative information on your credit report, you will be asked for an explanation. If your debts are too high when added to the new purchase or line of credit, your application may be denied.

As an individual, you can get a free copy (once a year) of your credit report from the credit reporting agencies. Another way a credit grantor evaluates your application is by assigning a certain number of points to specific categories. For example, points are assigned for the following: marital status, number of dependents, whether you own or rent your home, years of employment, credit history, monthly obligations, age, years at your current residence, years at your previous residence, occupation, monthly income, and other factors. The points are totaled. If you fall within the range that they accept, you'll get another green light and you'll be approved.

What You Need to Know About Your Credit Report

A credit grantor makes sure that you have revealed all the pertinent information it has requested. If there is any negative information listed in your credit report, such as charge-offs, collection accounts, slow payments, delinquent payments, tax liens, judgments, or bankruptcies, your application may be denied or further explanations may be required. In other words, you will have driven into a ditch, and you'll need help getting out and back on the road.

The Fair Credit Reporting Act allows credit entries, both good and bad, to stay on your credit report for up to seven years from the last date of activity. Bankruptcies can remain on your credit report for up to 10 years from the date they were filed or discharged.

When you cut up your credit cards, be sure to send the creditor, certified mail with a return receipt requested, a letter canceling your account. If you do not do this, your account will appear to be still active. Approximately three weeks after you send back your cut-up cards, request a copy of your credit reports to make sure the creditor has indicated that the account is closed.

Always get a copy of your credit report before you apply for new credit. There may be errors you need to correct before proceeding with your application. An incorrect report may result in your application being denied. Or if you're trying to rent an apartment and there are problems listed on your report, the landlord may increase the required deposit. On the other hand, if you are upfront about any credit problems, many creditors will work with you or show you what to do to reapply in the future.

It's important to understand the seriousness of paying amounts due on your credit cards or any loans you receive. You never want to be late making a payment; at the least, make the minimum payment on time. If you find that your payment is going to be late, call the creditor and explain your situation.

Find out the number of days that you can be late before it goes on your credit report. Don't wait to make a double payment the next month. If the past due payment rolls into the next billing cycle, most creditors automatically report a late payment on your credit report.

Finally, never apply for more credit than you need. Too many open and unused accounts will hurt your chances of getting new credit. Once you have established new credit, make sure you review your credit report once a year. Now that you've finished the first leg of your journey, let's see what's around the next turn in the road.

A Four-Way Intersection: Where to Turn to Establish Credit

There are several ways to establish credit: secured credit cards, merchant cards, credit cards cosigned by friends or relatives, and loans from automobile dealers. Let's take each method for a test drive.

Secured credit cards. Secured credit cards are an excellent way to establish credit. A bank offering a secured credit card requires that you deposit a certain amount of money into a savings account at its bank. In exchange for the deposit, you will be issued a Visa or MasterCard. The bank will pay you interest on the money you deposited into your savings account. The amount that you deposited will be your credit limit. Any purchase or charge that you make with the credit card will be charged interest.

For example, your deposit may be $500. A Visa or MasterCard is then issued to you with a credit limit of $500. You will receive a low rate of interest on the amount you deposited, but you will also be paying interest at a higher rate on on any credit card balance you accumulate. To avoid paying interest, pay the balance off every month because the amount of interest you will receive from the deposit is always less than the amount you will be charged for the balance you run.

As you use the card, you will receive a monthly statement. Again, try to pay the balance off in full, or at least make the minimum payment on time. As the payments are received, the bank will report the activity on your credit report. This report is important because you are building a payment pattern for future lines of credit. Many banks will issue you an unsecured credit card after you have been with them for 18 months. The key is making the payments on time. Stay in your driving lane and keep traveling toward your destination.

With a secured credit card, there may be an application fee and an annual fee. The interest rates are high, but it is a good way to establish or reestablish your credit. More and more banks are offering this type of program. Contact your local bank to see if they offer any secured credit card programs. You also can look in the business section of your newspaper to see if they have information on which banks offer secured credit cards.

Some individuals who have not had credit problems will still opt to have a secured credit card. They may deposit the maximum amount allowable into a savings account, draw interest on the balance, use the credit card, and pay the balance off each month. Many people find this is a good way to keep control of their own money and earn interest while doing it.

Merchant cards. If you've never had a credit card in your name, getting one from a local merchant will help you establish credit in the future, providing the store provides your payment history to the major credit reporting agencies. If the merchant is not a subscriber to these agencies (Experian, Trans Union, and Equifax), your payment history at that store will not be reflected on your credit report, and therefore it will not help you establish credit. When applying for credit for major credit cards and department store cards, or for credit at any type of lending institution, a credit report is always run to evaluate your paying history. So make sure the merchant is a subscriber to the reporting agencies.

Once you have a merchant card and have established a good payment history, you should apply for a Visa or MasterCard. Look for a low-interest credit card. Credit cards given by most merchants have high interest rates. Therefore, when you have one or two Visa or MasterCards, cancel your merchant and department store credit cards and only use the low-interest credit cards. Visa and MasterCard are accepted almost everywhere.

Credit cards cosigned by friends or relatives. If you're applying for your first credit card and you're just starting out in life, many credit card companies ask for a parent's signature on the credit application to make sure the payment will be made. In other words, your parent is guaranteeing your line of credit, which means that if you run up your bill and can't make the payments, the creditor will go after your parents to collect. This failure to pay will be reported on your parents' credit report as well as your own. And if there are any delinquencies or defaults on the account, both credit reports will reflect this, too. A cosigned card is similar to a "learner's permit" driver's license because the card gets you started on the road to credit. It is dissimilar in that someone else is responsible for paying for your mistakes.

There are two other ways that friends or relatives can help you establish credit in your name. Both involve having joint credit cards. Once a credit card is issued to an individual, the card issuer frequently allows the cardholder to request an additional card in another person's name. Ask your friend or relative to obtain a card in your name.

The first way to establish credit using this method is to tell your friend to keep your card because you won't be using it. In this way a positive credit rating will be established for you. The hazard is that your friend or relative needs to make the payments on time. If that's not possible, make sure your friend lets you know ahead of time so you can help. Remember, your friend's payments and nonpayments are going to show up on your credit report, so you have a vested interest in making sure that your friend can make those payments. Otherwise your credit report could be hurt by your friend's nonpayment. Clearly, this approach works best if you have a financially reliable friend or relative!

The second way to use this approach is for you to keep and use the credit card as long as your friend or relative doesn't mind you using the account. Then make sure you keep track of all of your purchases and make the payments on time. (It is even better if the credit card is used only by you, so your purchases will not be confused with the original cardholder.) Have the statement sent to your friend or relative. Make the payment to the credit card company on time. That way your friend or relative will feel secure.

Once you have established a good payment pattern on your credit report, apply for your own credit card. Have your friend or relative cancel the card with your name on it. If there is still an outstanding balance, make sure you continue to make the payments to reflect a good payment pattern.

First Time Buyer Auto Loans. You can also establish credit by buying or leasing a car. However, any time you respond to an ad for a first time buyer purchase for an automobile, always read the fine print. Make sure you understand how the program works. The car dealer may require a larger down payment or deposit for the car. You also will probably pay a higher interest rate than you would from a financial lender.

Make sure the loan company that the car dealer uses is a subscriber to the credit reporting agencies. If they are not, don't get the car. It is important that your payment history is reported to the credit reporting agencies.

If you complete the purchase and make payments on the car for at least 12 months, you can shop around for another lender that offers a lower interest rate and have the new lender refinance the car. Because you have been making your payments on time and show a good payment history, you have a good chance of refinancing the car and also establishing new credit with a major credit card. It's smooth driving now!

Finding Your Way to Major Credit Card Companies

Once you've established some credit, you can apply for a major credit card: Visa, MasterCard, American Express, or Discover. As mentioned, many of these companies solicit new customers. But if they haven't been looking to sign you up by sending you offers in the mail, then it's up to you to find them. The easiest way to do this is to go to each company's Web site: http://www.americanexpress.com, http://www.discover.com, http://www.mastercard.com, and http://www.visa.com.

For example, at the Visa Web site, you can learn about the credit cards Visa offers: Visa Classic, Visa Secured, Visa Gold, Visa Platinum, Visa Signature, Reward Cards, and smart Visa Cards. The company also offers a special credit card for students, a debit card (the Visa Check Card), and prepaid cards and products (Visa Gift Card). At this point, however, you want a basic credit card, such as the Visa Classic credit card, which the company Web site describes as an ideal first card because of its simplicity, flexibility, and worldwide recognition. Whether you're a student, a young couple, or someone trying to establish credit, apply now for the convenience of owning a Visa card. And if you don't have a computer or access to the Internet, you can always call each company. You can then ask for the information to be mailed to you.

A Fork in the Road: Credit Cards vs. Debit Cards

Now that banks have debit cards associated with Visa and MasterCard, some people are unsure whether it's better to make a purchase with a credit card or a debit card. There are different uses for each type of card. A debit card automatically pays a bill by deducting funds from your bank account. With your credit card, you create a bill, and the credit card has no connection to your bank accounts.

The primary reason to use a credit card is that your credit card account is not immediately debited. If you have a grace period with your account, you would have approximately 25 to 30 days to pay the charge with no interest. With the debit card, each charge is immediately withdrawn from your account.

On the other hand, debit cards are a good substitute for cash. They are more like checks than credit cards. To use a debit card, a proper point-of-sale system or point-of-purchase device must be available to electronically transmit the information on your card to the bank. The bank also credits the merchant's account immediately for the amount of the sale. One disadvantage of using a debit card is that your history of payments isn't reported on your credit report, whereas your payment activity on your credit card will be reported monthly.

Many credit card issuers also provide an ATM card to use as a charge card. However, as with a debit card, using the ATM card doesn't help establish credit, and it doesn't help your credit report. It won't be reported as a credit card. In fact, an ATM card is not a credit card. The cost of any purchases that you make with your ATM card, even if it has the Visa or MasterCard insignia on it, is directly taken from your checking or savings account. There is no bill sent to you at the end of the month to make payments on the purchases because the money was automatically taken from your account and paid to the merchant.

By using an ATM Visa card, you can keep better track of your purchases. It can be used the same way a credit card is used for reservations and purchases, but there is no billing other than the automatic transfer of the funds from your bank account to the merchant's account.

Ease on Down the Road but Not *Too* Easily

Once you obtain an application for a major credit card, consider the interest rates and annual fees before you accept an offer of credit. Let's kick the tires to see what the pitfalls are.

Interest charges. Before completing a credit application, read the disclosure of terms located somewhere in the application. The disclosure of terms will list the annual percentage rate (APR). For example, a loan may have an APR of 21 percent. To figure out the total cost in dollars of a car loan, for example, multiply your monthly payments by the total number of months of the loan. From the total payments, subtract the total amount borrowed to see how much you are paying in interest. For example, if you borrow $1,000 at an

APR of 21 percent, the APR adds $210 to the $1,000 loan, for a total of $1,210. To calculate your monthly payment, simply divide $1,210 by 12. This figure reveals that you need to pay $100.83 per month for one year.

For a credit card, some creditors calculate interest on a daily basis. That means that interest charges begin to accumulate as soon as a purchase or charge is made. Other creditors calculate interest on a prorated basis, giving you a grace period. That means no interest is charged until the billing cycle ends. The grace period could be 25 to 30 days from the purchase date. You can repay the amount you charged in full during the grace period with no interest charged. The best cards to use are those that have a grace period. You get free use of the money that you will be using to make the payment during the 25 to 30 days before the statement is due. The way to take full advantage of this form of payment is to pay the total balance off each month.

Always review your credit card application to see what the cost will be. If there is no grace period, look for another creditor who offers one. If you always pay your credit card balance in full, you want a grace period and no annual fee. You won't care what the APR is because you will never pay it!

Some credit card companies offer low-interest credit cards, but they are hard to qualify for. They require that you have a good payment history with no negative information and that you are not overextended. The creditor will look at your job stability, your income, and the length of time you have lived at your current address.

Before applying for a low-interest credit card, call the credit processing department and find out what the creditor's criteria is for qualification. Then ask which credit reports they run. Before applying, also get a copy of your credit report from all three credit reporting agencies: Experian, Trans Union, and Equifax.

If you know prior to making an application that you fit the criteria the creditor is looking for, follow through with the application. If you don't fit the criteria, make whatever improvements are necessary and apply at a later date. In other words, pull over to a rest stop and take a break; you can get back on the road later.

Annual fees vs. no fee cards. When you're first trying to establish credit, you may be offered only "subprime" credit cards. These differ from "prime" cards, which are generally offered to people who already have established good credit. The following are the differences between these two categories.

Subprime credit cards
- ▶ accept some bad credit
- ▶ have a higher interest rate
- ▶ offer a lower credit limit
- ▶ have a higher annual fee
- ▶ have higher "nuisance fees"
- ▶ offer no rewards
- ▶ may require application and set-up fees
- ▶ may have no grace period on purchases

Prime credit cards
- ▶ require good credit
- ▶ offer lower interest
- ▶ offer a higher credit limit
- ▶ have a lower or no annual fee
- ▶ have lower "nuisance fees" (late or over-limit fees)
- ▶ may offer rewards, such as frequent flyer points
- ▶ offer low-rate balance transfer offers
- ▶ offer convenience checks
- ▶ allow a grace period on purchases

Watch Out for Roadblocks: If You Are Denied Credit

If you apply for credit and are denied, don't give up and go home. You may not be on the fast track, but there are side streets you can take to get there. First, find out why you've been denied. There are several possible reasons, and many are easy to resolve or correct. Let's take a look at a few of these speed bumps.

Include all required contact information. Before you make your application, make sure you have all your travel documents in order. One simple problem is not including your phone number on your application, especially if it's unlisted. The lender needs to know that you can be contacted if you default on your payments. So be sure to include your number on the application.

Keep your credit history up to date. Another easy-to-fix problem can occur when you've had great credit in the past, but you've paid off all your balances on all your accounts and stopped using your cards. Most lending institutions and credit card companies will review your credit report, see

Hazard!

Don't Get Sideswiped by High Interest Rates: Read the Fine Print!

Credit card companies are always seeking new customers, and they use various enticements. They may offer a low interest rate or such incentives as airline miles, product discounts, long-distance telephone privileges, and offers to reestablish credit.

New customers run into problems when they don't read the fine print. For example, a credit card with a low interest rate usually requires you to move your balances from credit cards with higher interest rates to the new card. If you don't follow the guidelines, the company can increase the new card's interest rate so that it is even higher than your old card's rate! Because the lower interest rate is only temporary, you may find that unless you pay more than the minimum on the new card, you'll need several years to pay off your balance.

Another problem is accepting too many offers. It's easy to lose track of the credit cards you have. If you don't cancel the credit cards that you're not using, you may have trouble when you try to establish new credit. You risk sinking into more debt.

Consumer advocates blame banks and other credit card providers for the rising numbers of overextended consumers and bankruptcies. These institutions inundate consumers with more than 2 billion solicitations a year, which tempt individuals to live beyond their means. So watch out!

what accounts you had in the past, and look for your past 24 months' payment history, which indicates how stable your financial situation is and how you pay your bills. Once you pay off all your credit obligations, no payment history will be reported on your credit report, though the last date of activity will be included. And if there have been no payments made on any accounts within the past 24 months to show a payment pattern, many lenders will decline your application.

Therefore, when applying for credit, you need to know what a lender will look for in qualifying you for credit. Paying off your credit cards is great, but it's wise to keep one or two accounts open and pay the balances off each month. That way there will always be a payment pattern should you seek additional credit. Your credit history is like a current driver's license: You need it in case you get pulled over.

Hey, Bro!

I'm settling in to my new place and new job. So far, no problems except getting a credit card. Would you believe? My application was denied! I called to ask why, and customer service said they couldn't verify my telephone number. (It's unlisted.) Once I gave it, they called back and approved me. What's up with that?

It turns out many companies deny credit if your number's unlisted because you're harder to find if you stop paying. Many applications even request your current phone bill, which shows your number, name, and address. So if your number's unlisted, attach a copy of your bill to your application before they ask, to eliminate a delay or denial. Hopefully, you won't have the same problem I had!

Many applications also require you to list relatives or friends as references. If you stop paying and your credit goes into default, and you change your phone number or address so they can't locate you, they'll contact your references to find you. If you want to list me, let me know: I promise not to tell anything too personal (ha!)

Hope you're okay. Let me know if you'll be in town!

Make sure you meet all of the application's qualifications before you apply. Some people are denied even when they submit so-called preapproved applications, which seems contradictory. Unfortunately, most of these preapprovals aren't what they appear to be. You need to read the whole letter and the full application. The small print usually has a disclaimer stating the preapproval is subject to acceptance of the application, and the small print on the application states that you'll be approved subject to a credit report review and verification of information from the application.

There could be several reasons why you were denied the credit card. Your credit report may not reflect a good credit history. Your income may not be high enough. The credit report may show too much debt. Or you may not have lived at your current residence long enough.

A preapproved application will be reviewed using the same qualification factors as if you had solicited the application yourself. Never complete any application unless you have read every word in the letter and application. This habit will help you avoid sending in an application that you know will be turned down and eliminate an inquiry being placed on your credit report. Too many inquiries on your credit report can hurt your chances of future credit.

Apply when you're currently working and meeting the company's income requirements. The Fair Credit Reporting Act was recently changed to allow creditors to reject your preapproved credit card application if they conclude that you are unemployed or your income is not high enough. Formerly the company was required to make an offer of credit. The preapproved credit card usually has a high interest rate or a low credit limit.

The Fair Credit Reporting Act allows creditors to consider any substantial changes in your financial condition. This could be a sudden drop in your income or a sudden increase of debt. If anything should occur between the time you make application and the time the review application is reviewed, you can be denied.

Many credit institutions are replacing their preapproved offers with invitations to apply. Always read all the fine print on any solicitation to apply for credit. Many times the offer is not what it appears to be.

How to Request Your Credit Report

The Fair Credit Reporting Act gives guidelines on what credit reporting agencies can and can't do regarding consumers' credit reports. The credit reporting agencies are regulated by the Federal Trade Commission (FTC). Any complaints you have against a credit reporting agency should be directed to the FTC.

Understanding your credit reports can be a problem. With three major credit reporting agencies holding information on more than 160 million Americans, errors can happen. The information that is stored in the credit bureaus is data that the creditors report to the bureaus.

Many people are afraid to see what is in their credit reports, but fear should never stop you from requesting them. Lack of knowledge about what is reported about you can cause you embarrassment or shock when applying for credit. Even if you feel your credit record is immaculate, be sure of what your credit report says about you.

Approximately 70 percent of people who request credit reports find some inaccuracies being reported. The key is understanding your credit report and knowing what you can do about problem entries. For example, files are often mixed up if you have the same name as a parent (Bill Jones Sr., Bill Jones Jr., or Bill Jones I, II, or III), or if you have a common name such as John Smith.

Some people have also had accounts opened in their names without their knowledge. Credit fraud is not uncommon. All three credit reporting agencies (Experian, Trans Union, and Equifax) have special programs on their computers that show how many times there have been inquiries about your Social Security number and address. If this number is excessively high, someone may be trying to use your identification to get credit. By requesting your credit report at least once a year (preferably every six months) from the three reporting agencies, you can uncover any problems in your report and correct them before you request new credit.

Once you receive a copy of your credit report, review every entry, including your name, address, and Social Security number. Understanding your credit report can be confusing, but here are a few tips on how to read each company's report:

► Experian has made its reports easy for consumers to read. Each entry is numbered. A dash before and after the numbered entry indicates a negative entry.

► Trans Union puts all the negative entries on the first portion of your credit report. The negative entries have brackets (< >) around the creditors' names.

► Equifax codes its entries for payment history by using numbers one through nine. A number one is good; anything above that is negative. Carefully examine every entry to make sure it is correct.

Here's how to contact each company to get a copy of your credit report:

Trans Union
P.O. Box 390
Springfield, PA 19064
1-800-888-4213
http://www.transunion.com

Equifax
P.O. Box 740193
Atlanta, GA 30374-0193
1-800-685-1111
http://www.equifax.com

Experian
P.O. Box 2104
Allen, TX 75013
1-888-EXPERIAN (888-397-3742)
http://www.experian.com

Dear Sis,

Good news: I'm climbing my way out of debt! I know you were worried when I reached the credit limits on my cards, especially when the total hit $12,000. But the calculations you suggested helped. One card's balance was $2,000. By making only the minimum payment every month, it would have taken me 16 and a half years to pay it off, assuming I never made another purchase with that credit card. And the interest would have been $2,504.62. Adding the interest to the $2,000 would make a total of $4,504.62! No way could I afford that.

Then I recalculated and figured out that I can pay just $5 more per month than the minimum payment, which will save me $738.59 and eliminate more than five years from the loan. If I can pay $10 over the minimum, I can save $1,113.70 and eliminate eight years from the loan. I also have to avoid using the credit cards I'm paying down. When my balances are low enough, I'll start transferring the higher interest rate credit card balances to the lower ones and continue to add extra payments.

So thanks for the advice, and if you can spare a loan to help even more, let me know!

As mentioned, one copy is free per year; if you are requesting additional copies, enclose payment for each credit report. Include your name, address, Social Security number, date of birth, and a photocopy of your driver's license or utility bill that has your name and address listed.

Finally, if you have been turned down for credit, you can request a free copy of your credit report within 60 days of being denied the credit. In your letter, give the name of the creditor who denied your credit application.

Don't Drive Recklessly: How to Manage Your Debt

Now that you're on the road to establish your credit, let's talk about staying off the road to debt. In the United States, only about one-third of people with credit cards pay their balance in full each month. The other two-thirds carry a balance from one month to the next. The interest rate associated with this outstanding balance averages about 12 percent and can sometimes exceed 25 percent. Credit cards represent a major convenience for many people, but they have also become a significant burden for others.

Consumer debt is one of the biggest problems most people face. Credit allows you to buy something today by committing dollars you hope to earn in the future. By using credit, you are immediately reducing the amount of available money you will have next week, next month, and next year. Doesn't this strike you as a strategy that's the opposite of the one you'd like? Don't you actually want to have more money available next week, next month, and next year? Of course you do!

One of the biggest problems with credit card spending is that most people don't incorporate these purchases into their available monthly cash flow. As a result, purchases are made that often exceed an individual's monthly net income. Most people intend to pay the balance each month, but as the month rolls forward, they don't have the resources to do so, yet they always rationalize this spending. Because of the inherent problems and financial risks associated with credit card spending, many financial advisors and coaches suggest that their clients not use credit cards at all. If a card is needed to pay for a hotel visit, rental car, or airline flight, the safest card to use is a debit card, because the purchase is made from existing funds in your bank account.

Watch the Speed Limit: Don't Spend More Than You Really Have

The key to successful credit card spending is making sure you set aside an amount of money from your monthly net income equal to your credit card purchases, so you can pay the card balance in full each month. If you prefer to make purchases with a credit card, consider using an "envelope system" to manage your money. This method is how people used to manage their money years ago, before credit cards, debit cards, and ATM cards proliferated. People literally cashed their paychecks. (We don't even do that anymore; instead, we rely on direct deposit!) They then divided the cash into envelopes for each regular expenditure, including rent or mortgage, transportation costs, books and other entertainment costs, clothing, groceries, vacations and weekends away, medical and dental expenses, and so forth. Tollbooth 2.1 shows what this method looks like. The beauty of the system is that when you decide to use it, you commit to living within your means.

Although it is unlikely you will be using credit cards with a cash-based envelope system, you need to create a credit card repayment envelope for each credit card you use if you do decide to try this plan. Every time you buy something with your credit card, you take money from the appropriate envelope and place it in the credit card repayment envelope. For example, if you wanted to purchase an article of clothing from an Internet retailer for $45 using your Visa card, you would take $45 from your clothing envelope and place it in your Visa repayment envelope. When your Visa bill arrives,

Tollbooth 2.1

The Traditional Envelope Budgeting System

Cash from paycheck = $1200

Mortgage	Gas	Electrical	Vehicle	Groceries	Savings	Misc.
$400	$25	$75	$100	$150	$75	$25

Medical	Gifts	Donations	Taxes	Education	Vacation
$90	$25	$25	$125	$75	$10

Sum of envelopes = $1200

Sum of paycheck is equal to sum of envelopes

Tollbooth 2.2

Credit Card Repayment Using the Envelope Budgeting System

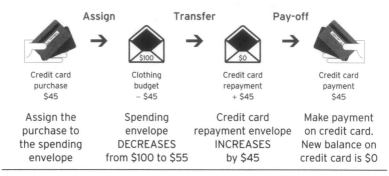

	Assign		Transfer		Pay-off	
Credit card purchase $45	→	Clothing budget – $45	→	Credit card repayment + $45	→	Credit card payment $45
Assign the purchase to the spending envelope		Spending envelope DECREASES from $100 to $55		Credit card repayment envelope INCREASES by $45		Make payment on credit card. New balance on credit card is $0

you will use the money in the repayment envelope to pay the entire balance, as shown in Tollbooth 2.2.

Don't Drive on Cruise Control: Pay Your Debts First

First of all, if you have credit card debt or personal loans, pay them off first. It does not make sense to carry a credit card balance and pay interest of 9.9 to 21 percent or more while you have cash sitting in a savings account earning 1 percent interest. Paying off the credit card debt is almost always the best return you can get on your money. Once your credit cards are paid off, use the money that you had been spending on monthly payments to build up your emergency fund (the cash you keep on hand in case of sudden major expense or loss of income).

If you have an existing balance on your credit card when you begin using the envelope system, and you don't have any savings to help pay it off, you need to allocate an amount of your monthly net income to meet the monthly payment requirements for that card. When you make your credit card payment, you will pay this monthly allocation and an amount that represents your total card purchases for the previous month. This approach allows you to begin reducing your credit card balance and ensures that future purchases are paid in full each month.

You can adapt the traditional envelope system to a ledger or spreadsheet that resembles the envelope method or to an automated software-based system. If you use a ledger or a spreadsheet, you need to create a repayment account for each credit card you intend to use. As credit card purchases are made, you should enter a transfer from the appropriate spending account to the credit card repayment account. Each month, credit card payments will be tracked on the corresponding repayment spending account ledger.

If you use a software-based envelope system, the repayment account is created during your initial setup. When credit card purchases are made, transfers from the selected spending account to the appropriate repayment envelope take place automatically as you make an assignment of the transaction in the program.

It's a lot easier to explain debt by looking at some scenarios from real life. Let's take two side trips to see what happens in two situations: when your expenses exceed your current income and when your expenses match your present income.

Debt Case Study #1: When Your Current Expenses Exceed Your Current Income

Suppose you want to buy a new entertainment center, with a large-screen TV, a DVD player, and a booming new stereo system for your new home. You shop around at discount electronics stores, but the best price you can find is $1,650. For this example, we called around to find out about financing plans, and the rate we were quoted was a whopping 20.65 percent. This means that on a $1,650 purchase, you would have to pay back at least 3 percent of the loan each month for a minimum payment of about $50 per month. Let's compare buying the set on credit and saving for the purchase. (See Tollbooth 2.3.)

Notice the difference in the number of months it takes to pay for your new entertainment center for each scenario. Using credit, it will take more than 47 months to pay off the loan. That's almost four years on a two-lane highway moving 45 miles per hour! In contrast, saving to make the purchase takes only 32 months, only two and a half years, which is just over one-half the time it would take using the credit card payment plan. Now you're on the turnpike where the traffic is going 80. And that's where you want to be.

In addition, if you pay for the entertainment center on credit, the overall cost of your entertainment center is $2,338.57 after you pay all of the interest charges, whereas the total cost is only $1,600 if you saved money for the

Tollbooth 2.3

Buying on Credit vs. Saving and Paying Cash

	Date	Payment	Interest*	Balance
1	04/01/06	50		1650
2	05/01/06	50		1600
3	06/01/06	50		1550
4	07/01/06	50		1500
5	08/01/06	50		1450
6	09/01/06	50		1400
7	10/01/06	50		1350
8	11/01/06	50		1300
9	12/01/06	50		1250
10	01/01/07	50		1200
11	02/01/07	50		1150
12	03/01/07	50		1100
13	04/01/07	50	283.94	1333.94
14	05/01/07	50		1283.94
15	06/01/07	50		1233.94
16	07/01/07	50		1183.94
17	08/01/07	50		1133.94
18	09/01/07	50		1083.94
19	10/01/07	50		1033.94
20	11/01/07	50		983.94
21	12/01/07	50		933.94
22	01/01/08	50		883.94
23	02/01/08	50		833.94
24	03/01/08	50		783.94
25	04/01/08	50	218.67	952.61
26	05/01/08	50		902.61
27	06/01/08	50		852.61
28	07/01/08	50		802.61
29	08/01/08	50		752.61
30	09/01/08	50		702.61
31	10/01/08	50		652.61
32	11/01/08	50		602.61
33	12/01/08	50		552.61
34	01/01/09	50		502.61
35	02/01/09	50		452.61
36	03/01/09	50		402.61
37	04/01/09	50	139.93	492.53
38	05/01/09	50		442.53
39	06/01/09	50		392.53
40	07/01/09	50		342.53
41	08/01/09	50		292.53
42	09/01/09	50		242.53
43	10/01/09	50		192.53
44	11/01/09	50		142.53
45	12/01/09	50		92.53
46	01/01/10	50		42.53
47	02/01/10	88.57	46.04	0
	Totals	2338.57	688.57	

	Date	Deposit	Interest	Balance
1	04/01/06	50		50
2	05/01/06	50		100
3	06/01/06	50		150
4	07/01/06	50		200
5	08/01/06	50		250
6	09/01/06	50		300
7	10/01/06	50		350
8	11/01/06	50		400
9	12/01/06	50		450
10	01/01/07	50		500
11	02/01/07	50		550
12	03/01/07	50		600
13	04/01/07	50	9.75	659.75
14	05/01/07	50		709.75
15	06/01/07	50		759.75
16	07/01/07	50		809.75
17	08/01/07	50		859.75
18	09/01/07	50		909.75
19	10/01/07	50		959.75
20	11/01/07	50		1009.75
21	12/01/07	50		1059.75
22	01/01/08	50		1109.75
23	02/01/08	50		1159.75
24	03/01/08	50		1209.75
25	04/01/08	50	28.04	1287.79
26	05/01/08	50		1337.79
27	06/01/08	50		1387.79
28	07/01/08	50		1437.79
29	08/01/08	50		1487.79
30	09/01/08	50		1537.79
31	10/01/08	50		1587.79
32	11/01/08	50	25.16	1662.95
	Totals	1600	62.95	1662.95

*Note that interest usually accrues at least monthly, not annually, but to simplify this example, we've used an annual calculation; in actuality, your total interest payments will be even *greater*.

purchase, because you would earn an additional $62.95 in interest on your savings. This illustration assumes, of course, that the purchase price doesn't increase over the 32 months. But even if the price increased 10 percent as a result of inflation, you would have to save for only an additional three months. The benefits are still clear: Buying on credit is a poor choice.

Of course, all of us want what we want right now, and this scenario doesn't take into consideration the fact that you have to save for two and a half years before you can buy all that new equipment. But the reality check comes at the end of the month when you're sitting at your desk full of bills and you're receiving a paycheck that never seems to be enough. Is that how you want to live for the rest of your adult life? No. And you don't have to go completely without. You can buy components of that entertainment center as you save: first the TV, then the DVD player, and so on. Think of this plan as going to a different country in Europe for 10 days every year: It may not be the same as traveling the entire continent for six months, but it's still a nice way to see some of the world!

Don't Carry Debt: This Is the #1 Money Problem Most People Have. None of us wants to live on the financial edge, but so many of us do and don't know what to do about it. So let's work on it. Stop reading right now and gather up every single bill you have, including fixed expenses, extra expenses, and all of your consumer debt, including credit card bills. Line up all of your debt obligations and list the names of the creditors, the current amounts you owe, the interest rates, and the minimum payments you are required to make. If you have read Chapter 1, you've already created a list of your expenses and debts in Roadmap 1.2, so this information should be readily accessible. Let's incorporate the data into a new chart in Tollbooth 2.4.

Next let's create a written plan of action. Tollbooth 2.5 offers hypothetical numbers that give you an example of how you might implement a debt reduction strategy into your overall budget plan. Imagine that you have the credit card and consumer debt shown in Tollbooth 2.5, which lists the balances you still have to pay, the interest rates, the amounts you've chosen to pay each month, and the remaining amount of time it will take for you to pay off each of these debts.

Several financial advisors have discussed a debt reduction strategy that they call "the snowball effect." It works like this: You organize all your bills in reverse order, listing those with the smallest balances first and moving down the list to the largest bill. Don't concern yourself with interest rates or

Tollbooth 2.4

List All Your Credit Card Debt

Whose name is on the account	Owed to/for	Balance owed	Months to pay off	Minimum payment	Interest

minimum payments; just stay focused on the road ahead. The new list would be rearranged as shown in Tollbooth 2.6.

Now that you've organized your bills, it's time to take control of them. First, you must begin to get ahead of the payments. To do that, you need a strategy that pays off the smallest balance in full. You must be able to generate some extra cash quickly, which may mean looking around for something to sell. How much money could you raise in a garage sale? Or could you work one day a week at a second job? Could you work some overtime? What could

Tollbooth 2.5

Hypothetical Debt Repayment Plan

	Balance	Interest Rate	Monthly Payment	Time Left
Credit Card #1	$ 3,000	11 percent	$ 77	4 years
Credit Card #2	1,500	14 percent	125	13 months
Car	9,000	9 percent	224	4 years
Gas Card	300	12 percent	50	6 months
Retail Store Card	600	16 percent	100	6 months
Home	90,000	7 percent	598	30 years

Tollbooth 2.6

A Better Debt Repayment Plan

	Balance	Interest Rate	Monthly Payment	Time Left
Gas Card	$ 300	12 percent	$ 50	6 months
Retail Store Card	600	16 percent	100	6 months
Credit Card #2	1,500	14 percent	125	13 months
Credit Card #1	3,000	11 percent	77	4 years
Car	9,000	9 percent	224	4 years
Home	90,000	7 percent	598	30 years

you do to earn enough money to pay off your smallest credit card bill? In this example, you need $300 to pay off the smallest balance. Whatever you do to pay off the first balance will set off a snowball effect that will bring you great pride if you are willing to stick to your plan. You're back on track!

After you pay off the $300 gas card in full, you have $50 of additional money to begin to increase your payments on the retail store card. By paying $150 a month, you'll pay off that bill in four months instead of six months! Then take the extra $150 a month and use that money to make payments on credit card #2, which you would then pay off in eight months instead of 13 months. You are now able to take the extra $275 a month and add it to the $77 for a total of $352 a month, which will allow you to pay off credit card #1 in a total of six months. Paying off a card is like passing the car in front of you: You're in the fast lane again!

You next work to pay off your car. Adding the $352 to your current payment of $224 will give you a whopping $576 a month to begin to carve away that debt. If you are able to stick to this plan, your car will be paid off in only a year. Tollbooth 2.7 shows the details and how you can zoom ahead to get rid of your debt.

This means you have paid off a total of $14,400 of debt in approximately 28 months, rather than over a four-year period. At the end of the 28 months, you have freed up a total of $576 a month, which can now be used to make additional principal payments on your home. Or you can use the money to save for a new car or for anything else you want to buy or save for, such as your retirement!

Tollbooth 2.7

A Fast-Track Debt Repayment Plan

	Current	1 month	4 months	8 months	16 months	28 months
Gas Card	$ 50	$ 0	$ 0	$ 0	$ 0	$ 0
Retail Store Card	100	150	0	0	0	0
Credit Card #2	125	125	275	0	0	0
Credit Card #1	77	77	77	352	0	0
Car	224	224	224	224	576	0
Home	598	598	598	598	598	598
Totals	$1,174	$1,174	$1,174	$1,174	$1,174	$598

How would an additional $576 of free cash flow a month make you feel? Probably great! You're in the driver's seat, and you're burning up the road! Debt reduction should be a priority goal. In this example, it would take just over two years to accomplish. But it requires commitment, persistence, and discipline. For 28 months, you might feel as though you're not making progress because you're choosing to take the savings and increase the payments on your remaining debt. Debt is a choice: You must make a decision not to use tomorrow's money to purchase today's pleasures.

Debt Case Study #2: When Your Current Expenses Meet Your Current Income

Living from paycheck to paycheck is a common situation, and unfortunately, it's how most Americans live. They can usually meet their monthly obligations, but they don't have an investment plan for their future, and they have little or no money in a savings account should any unexpected expenses arise. They're lurching down life's highway in a stick shift with a broken transmission.

This scenario is not a desperate situation, but almost all people want to have greater financial security. How we feel on an emotional level is very important. If a feeling of panic arises when you get sick or the car breaks down, both of which will happen at some point, and you are wondering where you will find the money to pay your doctor or your mechanic, then it is important to consider taking some of the steps listed above.

Most people who live from paycheck to paycheck plan to stay in the home they're living in or move to a bigger one. They also hope to continue driving the same car, but they are probably also burdened with several credit card payments that are infringing on their ability to build up a savings account. Therefore, if this is your situation, it's wise to focus on reducing your debt and other small expenses to free up the additional money necessary to begin to fund your financial plan. In other words, make a U-turn to Chapter 1 and review your budget, then take another look at Tollbooths 2.5 through 2.7!

Don't Drive Into a Ditch: Some Final Words of Advice

The best way to improve your credit and your credit score when you have credit cards with high account balances is to pay off the debt, and then keep the balances low enough to pay the cards off each month. If a card's limit is $2,000, and you have a balance of $1,800, the account's debt-to-credit ratio is 90 percent. A general guideline is to have no more than 40 percent debt-to-credit for each account. Pay down your credit cards with the smallest balance first, then those with the highest interest rates. Always remember: If you only pay the minimum payment each month, you'll never get out of debt. You're still on the road, but you're driving with the emergency brake on and you're not going anywhere. But if you manage your debt and maintain good credit, you'll find the road to your goals will lead to much smoother driving.

Learn the Language

Key Terms to Know When Dealing with Your Credit

Annual fees Fees charged by the bank that issues your credit card. Some banks charge nothing. Other companies charge a modest fee of $35 per year as a membership in its rewards program (in which you get reward points for using your card, which can then be redeemed for airline tickets, hotels, car rentals, and merchandise). Some companies such as American Express charge fees as high as $395 per year (platinum card), which offers many benefits, including no preset spending limits as well as travel, hotel, dining, and shopping privileges and rewards. Keep in mind, however, that you're still paying fees for these "rewards" and "benefits."

Annual percentage rate (APR) The interest rate you pay each year on an unpaid loan or credit card balance.

Cosigner An individual who signs for a loan (or credit card application) and assumes equal liability for the debt.

Credit history A record of how a person has repaid debts.

Credit rating An evaluation by a creditor or credit reporting agency to reflect a debtor's credit history based on payment patterns.

Finance charges The dollar amount paid to obtain credit. These fees are what your credit card issuer (the bank or other company that has granted you a credit card such as Visa or MasterCard) charges when you carry a balance rather than paying your entire credit card balance in full each month.

Grace period The period of time during which the credit card company will not charge interest on your purchases, usually until the end of that credit card's monthly billing cycle. Most companies offer a 25- to 30-day grace period, so you can repay the amount you charged in full during the grace period, with no finance charges.

Joint account An account that two or more people can use, with all parties assuming the responsibility to repay the debt.

Late fees Fees incurred when your credit card company receives your payment after the due date. Many credit card companies charge $20 per incident, and often even more.

Minimum payment The lowest amount you are required to pay on your total credit card balance. The minimum payment is usually very low—for example, something less than 5 percent of the total balance.

Secured credit card A credit card you can obtain by opening up a savings account with a bank offering this program. The bank will issue a major credit card, such as Visa or MasterCard, and secure it with your deposit. The amount of your line of credit will match what's in your savings account.

Win the Race

Getting the Most Out of Your Employer

Congratulations! You have a budget, you've set clear financial goals for yourself, and you've established credit that you can manage. During all that financial planning, you probably noticed that one big element of your financial life kept resurfacing: your income. Employee benefits are a large part of your income.

If you're currently employed, you should be maximizing your use of all of the benefits your company offers. If you're in the lucky position of weighing multiple job offers, or if you're considering changing jobs, you need to think about a potential employer's total financial package before making any move. Of course, comparing a salary, an annual bonus, and a commission plan are pretty much a no-brainer, so there's nothing there that you can't figure out on your own. Because the technical language of a company's benefits plan can seem like mumbo-jumbo at times (see "Learning the Language" at the end of this chapter), this chapter's road trip describes the value of a company's benefits plan, and by value, we do mean financial value.

Most large corporations and many smaller companies offer lots of benefits that can have a huge impact on your financial situation. Among the plans available are 401(k) investment plans, which can help you save toward your retirement, and health insurance, life insurance, tuition reimbursement, and flexible spending plans. This chapter covers all of these benefits and more, and it helps you evaluate not only your current employment situation but also how to assess the value of these benefits when you consider moving on to a new job.

Whether you work for a large or a small company, a nonprofit organization, a for-profit firm, or a government agency, the package of employee benefits available to you is crucial in putting together your personal financial plan. It takes a little time and effort to understand your benefits package, but if you fully utilize it, you will be in much better financial shape than if you toss your employee benefits handbook in a drawer and vow to yourself, "I'll get to it as soon as I can."

Although your employee benefits or human resources department provides printed brochures, pamphlets, and sometimes online information that explain your benefits, the initiative of reading and understanding the material rests with you. Your company provides the map, but you're in charge of learning how to read it and determining the route to your financial destiny.

More than 70 percent of Americans with the option to open a 401(k) account at work don't take full advantage of this fantastic wealth-building program. Millions of employees work their entire careers without talking to anyone from the employee benefits department until the day they retire or otherwise leave the company. By that time, of course, it is far too late to maximize the value of employee benefits. The best time to begin is when you first join a company. The earlier you enroll in certain programs, particularly retirement savings programs, the more time your assets will have to grow and help you meet your financial goals.

Okay, admit it. Retirement must feel like a million years away, so far down the road that you don't even want to bother with it now. But even if it is 40 or more years off, you still need to start thinking about it, even when you're just starting out. That's because of the beauty of compound interest: If you can put aside just the smallest amount of money now, it will earn so much interest later that you won't believe it. Let's take a quick detour and see how.

▶ Destination Retirement: The Benefits of Starting Early

The best way to maximize your assets is to begin contributing to your company retirement plan as soon as possible. The longer that money compounds, the more funds you will have at retirement. To illustrate this point dramatically, the employee benefits consulting firm of Kwasha Lipton in Fort Lee, New Jersey, compiled the chart shown in Tollbooth 3.1.

Kwasha Lipton assumes that you will save $1,000 a year, starting at age 25, 35, 45, and 55, and earn 9 percent a year on your savings until you retire at age 65. As indicated in the chart, you will accumulate $337,882 if you begin saving at age 25, $136,308 if you begin at 35, $51,160 if you begin at 45, and only $15,193 if you begin at age 55.

Over the long run, it can also pay to be more aggressive with your investments because each percentage point can mean thousands of extra dollars in your pocket at retirement.

Now that you know more about the benefits of saving and investing early, let's get back on the main highway and look at some specific types of retirement savings programs. In general, these programs are divided into two classes: a defined benefit plan and a defined contribution plan. Companies offer one or the other, and the next sections describe these two forks in the road.

Tollbooth 3.1

Amount of Money Available for Retirement

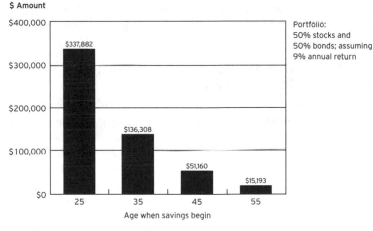

$ Amount

Portfolio:
50% stocks and
50% bonds; assuming
9% annual return

Age when savings begin

Source: Reprinted by permission of Kwasha Lipton, Fort Lee, New Jersey.

A Fork in the Road to Retirement: The Traditional Defined Benefit Pension Plan

The basic idea behind a traditional defined benefit pension plan is that your employer sets aside a certain amount of money in a trust fund for each employee every year. When you retire, the plan pays you a monthly pension benefit, usually based on the length of time you've worked at the firm and the salary level you've attained at the time you retire. Your employer not only puts up all of the money that goes into the pension fund, but it also hires money managers to invest it for both capital growth and regular income, which is distributed to pensioners (that means you).

Pension money is taxed only when it is paid to you, usually in fixed monthly installments. When you retire, you must report it as regular income in the year you receive it. Today many defined benefit plans also offer the option of a lump-sum distribution, which is described later in this section.

Mileage: The Farther You Travel, the More You Get

To qualify for pension benefits, you must work at a company long enough to become *vested*. Being vested means that you have given enough years of service (usually about 5 years) so that you have the legal right to receive some or all of your benefits when you reach retirement age, even if you no longer work for that employer. The number of years varies depending on the plan. Earning a year of service normally requires working at least 1,000 hours that year, or the equivalent of about 20 hours a week. These hours include the hours you were paid or were entitled to be paid, including vacation days, sick days, and back-pay days.

The Other Fork in the Road to Retirement: The Defined Contribution Plan

A properly invested defined contribution plan gives you the opportunity to accumulate an enormous amount of capital to enjoy at retirement. Unlike a defined pension plan, a contribution plan gives you plenty of choices and responsibility. For example, you must decide how much of your salary to contribute and how to invest the money among several options. If your selections prove profitable, you can end up with far more money at retirement than you ever dreamed possible. However, if you invest poorly, you must live with the consequences of having a retirement that is not as financially secure as it might have been.

Dear Liz,

We're having a great time here at the Grand Canyon. We were so pleased to hear you got the job you wanted, and at the salary you were negotiating for! The company 401(k) plan also sounds terrific,  *and you should start contributing to it as soon as you can. Investing in a 401(k) was the best advice your father and I ever received as newlyweds. In 1978, I invested at the lowest percentage level, but I increased it every time I got a raise. When my raise was 4 percent, I increased my contribution by 2 percent and still had a 2 percent raise in my paycheck (actually more, because of tax savings). Dad and I didn't miss that money because it was taken out before it ever reached our bank account. After only 11 years, I maxed out at the 16 percent level, and we never stressed our budget. We were able not only to save for your college tuition but were also able to look forward to our own financially secure retirement.*

We'll be home soon with fabulous pictures of our trip. 'Til then, congratulations!

Love, Mom

Multiple Lanes Ahead: Types of Defined Contribution Plans

Several types of defined contribution plans exist. In some cases, an employer contributes to its plan each year based on the firm's profitability. The better your company does, the bigger its contribution to your account. If the firm loses money one year, it may contribute nothing.

In other cases an employer provides a plan, but makes no contributions. Instead, contributions must be made entirely by employees on a voluntary basis. Most plans provide some mix of the two types, with employers matching employee contributions to a greater or lesser extent. When you reach retirement, you can either roll over the accumulated funds contributed by both you and your employer to an IRA or convert the assets into an annuity to be paid out (typically monthly) over the rest of your life. The main types of defined contribution plans are described in the following sections.

Employee stock ownership plan. Commonly called an ESOP, such a plan allows you, as an employee, to share in the profits of your company. Your company's contributions and your own are invested in company stock, which gives you and other employees more incentive to work diligently and help your company prosper. You should participate in an ESOP only if you believe your company has a solid long-term future. ESOP funds are not diversified because they are all invested in your company's stock, so you could take a big loss if your company falters.

Money Purchase Pension Plan. With a money purchase plan, your employer is obligated to contribute a set amount of your salary to the plan each year whether profits are up or down. When you retire, your monthly benefit payment is based on the amount that has accumulated in the plan.

Profit-Sharing Plan. This type of plan requires that your company contribute a certain percentage of your salary to the plan each year, depending on the firm's profits. This may amount to as much as 15 percent to 20 percent of your income in an extremely profitable year, or as little as nothing if the company lost money or earned anemic profits. Keep in mind, however, that most PSPs are discretionary—so a company could have large profits and still not contribute to its PSP. Profit-sharing plan assets can be invested in company stock, widely diversified stock, bond and money market funds, real estate, or insurance programs.

401(k) and 403(b) Plans. These plans allow you to defer a certain percentage of your salary (now up to 100 percent) to a tax-deferred account and invest the money in mutual fund–like accounts investing in stocks, bonds, or money market funds.

These programs allow you to contribute pretax dollars to a plan. In other words, the money you invest is taken off the top of your salary, and the amount of income reported to the IRS on your W-2 form is reduced by that amount. You only pay income taxes on these assets years later when you withdraw money from the plan in retirement.

This pretax feature makes these retirement plans far superior to other defined contribution plans, which are funded with dollars remaining *after* you have paid federal, state, local, and Social Security taxes. You are currently limited to a total annual contribution of $15,000 ($20,000 if you are 50 or older). This limit increases slightly each year in line with inflation.

In addition to the benefit of pretax funding, many companies match your plan contributions to some degree, either in cash or in company stock, making the deal even sweeter. The most generous companies match your contributions dollar for dollar, giving you a 100 percent return before the money is even invested. Many others match your contributions at 25 or 50 percent. Either way, these matching contributions are a terrific way to build your retirement plan. It's extra money given to you by your employer!

FYI: You can withdraw funds from a 401(k) or 403(b) account before you are age 59½, but according to IRS rules, you can do so only in the case of a well-defined financial hardship. This means that you must have an immediate need for funds for one of the following reasons:

► to pay for a major medical expense
► to purchase a home as a primary residence
► to avoid eviction from your apartment or foreclosure on your mortgage
► to cover post-secondary education expenses

You must prove not only that you have these expenses, but also that you have no other resources with which to pay them. However, most plans allow you to borrow against your plan's assets at a reasonable interest rate, so it makes little sense to withdraw the assets unless it is an emergency, and you see no way to pay back a loan.

Clearly, there are enormous benefits to having a 401(k) plan as a savings vehicle, including immediate tax savings on contributions, tax-deferred growth of investment earnings, and the possibility of free money in the form of matching contributions from your employer. Think of these three benefits as scenic views of what your retirement might be like, and let's take a look at them, with some real scenarios.

1. *Immediate Tax Savings.* Contributions to a 401(k) are withheld before taxes, and the plan grows with earnings tax-deferred. Think of these as toll-free roads! As with all qualified retirement plans, however, you suffer a 10 percent penalty if you withdraw money from the plan before you reach age 59½, and you must begin taking out money once you've

turned age 70½. So let's say you invest $100 per month annually in your company's 401(k) plan. Assuming you're in the 28 percent tax bracket, that's a little more than $320 in taxes owed on this amount if it's not contributed to the plan. In other words, your $1,200 investment in the 401(k) really costs you only about $880 when you account for the tax savings. To learn more about how pretax contributions can affect your take-home pay, visit http://www.401k.com/401k/tools/takehomepay/takehomepay.htm and click on 401k.com and follow the links.

2. *Tax-Deferred Growth.* Because interest and dividends in a 401(k) are tax-deferred, they compound tax free until you withdraw your investment. Over time the gap between the value of a taxable and a tax-deferred account, earning the same rate of return, increases sharply. To see how sharply, check out the differences shown in Tollbooth 3.2.

3. *The Employer's Match.* One of the greatest advantages of a 401(k) is that many employers contribute to their employees' 401(k)s by matching a portion of the money contributed by you, the employee. For example, for each $100 you contribute to the plan, your employer may add $50 to your account, giving you a total of $150. That's an immediate 50 percent return on your out-of-pocket $100 investment. No tax advantage gives you a better deal!

If a 401(k) plan is available, do whatever you can to invest in it, even if it's only a nominal amount from each paycheck. The maximum pretax contributions you can make to your 401(k) plan in 2006 is $15,000 ($20,000 for those age 50 and over). The limits also apply to 403(b)s for nonprofit workers; 457s for state and local government workers; and specialized SEPs, also known as 408(k) plans.

4. *Thrift savings plan.* With a thrift savings plan, you as an employee can contribute a certain percentage of your salary on an after-tax basis to the plan. The money can be invested in mutual fund–like accounts investing in stocks, bonds, money market funds, GICs (guaranteed investment contracts, similar to CDs), or company stock. The corporation may or may not match your contributions, depending on how company profits fare and how much the firm wants to promote the plan. Usually the company's matching funds must remain in an investment they require, such as company stock or a GIC. The company is under no obligation to contribute or match your investment.

Tollbooth 3.2

Comparison of Savings in a Tax-Deferred Retirement Account vs. a Taxable Account

This chart shows the results* of investing $100 a month in a tax-deferred retirement plan versus a taxable investment, subject to a 28 percent federal income tax rate.

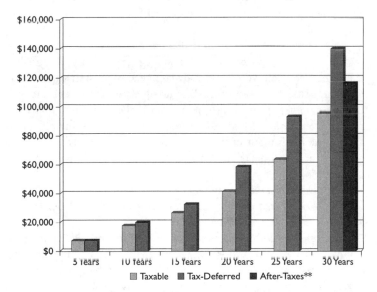

*Investment assumes the following: an annual effective 8 percent return, no changes to principal, and no change to the income tax rate.
**Tax-deferred investment after taxes. Although accumulations in a tax-deferred retirement plan are for retirement, we have illustrated the taxes you would pay on a lump-sum withdrawal after 30 years, given the assumptions. Payout options over time can spread out tax liability.

Defined Contribution Plans Offer Great Mileage

Participating in a defined contribution plan offers a number of advantages.

1. *It is fairly painless to contribute because the money is deducted automatically from your paycheck.* When you never see the money, doing without it is easier!

2. *You automatically use dollar cost averaging because you invest the same dollar amount every paycheck.* Dollar cost averaging is an investment method in which your dollars buy more shares when prices are down and fewer shares when prices are up, giving you an overall lower cost for your shares over time.

3. *You pay no brokerage commissions and your employer generally absorbs all the costs of administering the program.* If you choose to have your money invested in mutual fund–like accounts, the return you receive will be net of the professional management costs of approximately 0.5 to 1 percent.

4. *Any company match of your contributions boosts your return dramatically.* If your company contributes $.50 for every dollar you contribute to a retirement plan, you are already far ahead of most investors. What other investment pays an immediate tax-deferred 50 percent return?

5. *Many plans offer several investment options, allowing you to tailor your portfolio to your needs and risk tolerance.* You can also transfer money among the investment options, sometimes as frequently as daily but generally at least quarterly. (This strategy is discussed in more detail later in this chapter.)

6. *You can save a tremendous amount of money through pretax contributions and the tax-deferred accumulation of funds in a defined contribution plan.*

7. *Defined contribution plans can be sources of inexpensive loans.* Most companies allow you to borrow against the value of your plan, often at an interest rate of one percentage point higher than the prime rate. Paying back the loan is also easy because it is accomplished through payroll deduction over a period as long as five years. However, you are limited to the lesser of one-half of your account balance or $50,000.

Mileage: The Farther You Travel the More You Get

You may lose some or all of the company's matching or profit sharing contributions if you leave the company. Rules vary widely by company, but usually a company's matching funds become vested only after a specified period. For example, you might have to wait two or three years before each year's matching funds are yours to keep. In other companies, your benefits might become fully vested after you stay at the firm at least seven years. This delay is intended to deter you, the valued employee, from leaving the corporation soon after you sign on. No matter how long you have worked at a company, however, you become fully vested when you reach normal retirement age.

Extra Mileage: Current Tax Savings

As mentioned earlier, participation in a 401(k) or 403(b) plan not only generates tax-deferred retirement funds but also lowers your current tax bill because your contributions come off the top of every paycheck. As a result you avoid paying federal, state, and local income taxes on the money. This benefit in itself is a big boost, which is magnified when you add any matching funds your company contributes.

The following simple example, provided by the employee benefits consulting firm of Hewitt Associates, compares the investment that a 401(k) plan offers to the investment that you can amass on your own after taxes.

Suppose you earn $40,000 a year and contribute 6 percent of your salary or $2,400 to the plan. Your company matches your contribution $.30 on the dollar.

This example understates the advantages of 401(k) or 403(b) plans because the tax savings are much greater if you also include all the state and local income taxes you are able to avoid. In addition, if you invest the money on your own, the earnings on your after-tax investment of $2,400 would be taxed every year in the future, whereas your retirement plan balance would grow tax deferred until you withdraw the money at retirement.

When you combine the advantages of tax-deferred compounded savings and matching company contributions, the results can dramatically outperform the savings you could accumulate on your own with after-tax dollars.

Map Your Route: Asset Allocation

Once you've decided to participate in a defined contribution plan, the next task is to determine how to allocate your assets in the plan among the many investment options presented by your employer. This decision is intimidating to so many people that an entire industry has been founded solely to give people advice on allocating their employee plan benefits. Although you might seek help from these consultants, who often charge $180 an hour or more, you must ultimately decide the route that is best for you, and how it might change over time.

The first step in determining the proper mix of investments is to examine your entire portfolio, including your employee benefit plans, any other retirement plans you may already have (IRAs and Keogh accounts, described later in this chapter), and any other investment holdings you may have outside of your employee plans.

Next decide how you want to distribute your assets among broad categories of investments. For example, you might decide to keep 60 percent of your assets in stocks, 30 percent in bonds, and 10 percent in cash vehicles. Your task is to rearrange your portfolio so you end up with roughly this allocation. (Keep in mind that company retirement plans invest in mutual funds that, in turn, invest in pools of stocks and bonds, *not* directly in individual stocks or bonds.) In general, financial advisors agree that the younger you are, the more aggressively you should invest because of all the earning years ahead of you. Nevertheless, you must factor in your tolerance for risk.

In other words, are you more of a convertible sports car driver, or do you prefer a comfortable car that just gets good mileage? If you have some ability (emotionally, that is) to withstand the ups and downs of the stock market, invest more of your money in growth stocks. If you are frightened by the possibility of any capital loss, scale back the portion of your assets going into stocks. However, do not eliminate stocks from your portfolio altogether because you will cut out your best chance for long-term growth. Most people keep too much of their money in bonds or GICs, which are safer but offer limited growth potential.

Another asset in which people invest too much of their money is their own company's stock. Even if you believe your company is a wonderful place to work and has a great future, take advantage of the diversification options your benefit plans offer. When you tie up too much of your entire net worth in one company, you expose yourself to great danger if anything negative happens to the firm. You already have made a big commitment to your firm by choosing it as your employer. Take the opportunity your company gives you to branch out by investing in stock funds that may own shares in hundreds of companies.

The precise allocation of assets at any particular time depends on interest rates, stock and bond prices, and the outlook for the economy. For example, if interest rates are falling, you might want to keep more of your money in stocks, which are helped by falling rates, and less of your money in GICs and money funds, which pay lower returns as rates drop.

On the other hand, if interest rates begin rising, you might want to pull some money out of stocks and invest it in GICs and money funds. The general strategy remains consistent, however. Take more risk with your money when you are young and able to bounce back from temporary downswings in the stock market. As you near retirement, scale back your growth stocks in favor of more stable income-producing assets. By the time you reach retirement age, you'll have a more pleasant decision to make: how you should receive all the benefits you accumulated throughout your career.

Another Fork in the Road to Retirement: More Options

If you don't work for a major corporation that offers a defined benefit or defined contribution plan, that doesn't mean you can't have a retirement savings plan of your own. If you run or work for a small business or if you are self-employed, you have three options:

1. a simplified employee pension (SEP) plan
2. a savings incentive match plan for employees (SIMPLE)
3. a Keogh plan

All three of these programs offer some of the same tax advantages as defined contribution plans, including tax-deferred accumulation of investment earnings until retirement. They also offer similar investment and payout options. Roth IRAs and traditional IRAs are also great options. Appendix B lists resources with more information on these options; for now, let's stay on the main highway and find out more about how to get the most out of your employer.

▶ Tuition Reimbursement: On the Road Back to School

As the increasingly competitive workplace makes it more and more important for employees to sharpen their skills, many companies offer incentives for workers to return to school. Part of your education may be formal training classes held at your company for employees learning to operate a new piece of equipment, for example. Although these in-house classes don't offer any immediate financial benefit, they may make you more marketable for your next job, which can lead to a higher starting salary at your next company.

If you're interested in financial savings on education, that's available, too. Some companies pay most or all of the tuition at outside schools for classes directly related to your ability to keep or enhance your performance on your job. Many companies also reimburse most or all of your tuition if you can show that courses relate to a direction your career might take in the future. Finally, many firms also partially repay you for courses unrelated to your job. Most companies pay a portion of your tuition, not the entire amount, though reimbursement can range from 25 to 75 percent of your tuition costs. Typically you will receive 50 percent of the tuition for unrelated courses.

Other companies have strict policies that outline how much they'll pay and how they'll pay it. For example, employers may reimburse you 75 percent for degree and certificate programs, up to $3,000 per employee per calendar year; or 50 percent for personal growth and development coursework, up to $1,000 per employee per calendar year, using the institution's tuition deferral policy as the preferred method.

Different companies set varying requirements for tuition reimbursement. Some firms insist that you only pass the course; others reimburse you according to your grade (100 percent for an A, 80 percent for a B). Most companies require that you receive at least a B grade in order to be reimbursed; any grade lower than this, you foot the entire bill. In some cases, employers pay the school directly; in most cases you must put out your own money, and your firm will reimburse you at the end of the term when you prove that you have completed the course satisfactorily.

If you receive education assistance, it is not considered taxable income unless your tuition bills exceed $5,250 per year. If you spend your own money on books, lab fees, tutors, travel, or other extras, you can take a personal deduction on your tax return if your employer does not reimburse you for these costs.

Other forms of education assistance that employers provide are cash awards, scholarships, loans, and grants. Your company might pay for you to attend business school, for example, and also grant you paid or unpaid leave to complete the program. Many companies also offer scholarship programs for the children of employees, as well as various contests that offer thousands of dollars toward college tuition.

▶ Health Insurance Benefits: Fasten Your Seat Belt!

Although retirement savings programs are critical for your long-term financial needs down the road, health coverage has a greater impact on you now, particularly if you need frequent medical attention. In 2004, 84.3 percent of the U.S. population has health insurance, which leaves 15.7 percent or 45.8 million Americans without it. Company-provided health care today can be compared to the car you buy: Your seatbelt and driver's air bag come standard, but everything else is an option you'll need to pay for.

Today there are many health care options, but depending on the plan, there are deductibles, co-payments, out-of-pocket expenses, and paperwork. Despite the complexity, having medical coverage is crucial because the cost of health care is so high that even a minor procedure can take a major bite out of your budget. Serious surgery and extended recovery can cost tens to hundreds of thousands of dollars and wipe you out financially if you are uninsured.

Even preventive care and maintenance drugs can be expensive, although they're generally cost-effective because they prevent slight health problems from escalating into major ones. Because medical costs have risen so sharply in recent years, medical insurance premiums paid by employers have also skyrocketed, forcing companies either to cut back on coverage or boost the contributions employees make toward that insurance.

There are two basic kinds of health coverage:

1. traditional *fee-for-service plans*, in which the services provided by a doctor or another health care professional are paid in full or in part either directly to the provider or to you by an insurance company.
2. *prepaid plans*, such as health maintenance organizations (HMOs), in which your employer pays an insurance company a fixed fee for each employee, and you can use the HMO as much as you need to without paying much for each visit.

There are also "point of service" plans, which offer a hybrid of HMO and traditional plans, in which the patient can choose to be treated by the HMO or go out of network and be reimbursed at 70 percent instead of 80 percent. This type of plan has higher deductibles for out-of-network costs than the traditional plan does.

When an employer offers a health plan, it usually covers all employees as well as their spouses and children, though employees are required to contribute at least part of the premium, usually through an automatic payroll deduction. Employers with 50 or fewer employees and the self-employed can take advantage of health savings accounts (HSAs), which allow employees to put aside money out of their paychecks on a pretax basis to be used to pay health expenses or health insurance premiums. Employees are eligible to participate in these plans if they are only covered by a high-deductible health plan.

How Fee-for-Service Plans Work: Plan Your Own Tour

If your company contracts with a health insurer, you or your doctor submits all bills directly to the insurance company. The insurance company reimburses you for each procedure or expense (including drug prescriptions under some plans) based on either a fixed schedule of fees or on what is known as *usual, customary, and reasonable charges*. These terms mean that if your doctor charges more than the insurance company considers reasonable, you must pay the difference.

Deductibles. Most health insurance plans require that you pay a deductible each year before the insurance company begins to reimburse your expenses. For example, one insurance company plan might impose a $200 deductible, which means that you must pay 100 percent of the first $200 in medical expenses. You do not receive any cash back for your first $200 in medical claims.

Co-Payments. Even after you've met the deductible, most insurers will not reimburse you for your total bill. Typically, an insurer will compensate you for 80 percent of a doctor's charges, and you must cover the other 20 percent. In other words, if your doctor bill is $100, your insurance company will pay $80. You must pay the remaining $20 after you've paid the deductible, of course.

Out-of-Pocket Maximums. Fortunately, most traditional health insurance plans set a limit on how much you have to pay out for co-payments each year. The insurance company keeps track of how much you spend, and after you hit the out-of-pocket maximum, the insurer will pay 100 percent of your medical bills. This maximum is designed to protect you from financial hardship brought on by a series of large medical bills. Many companies set a dollar amount limit, such as $2,500 a year for employees and $5,000 for employees and their families.

Reimbursement Limits. In addition to setting deductibles and out-of-pocket maximums, most plans limit the total amount of money that the health insurance company will pay you. Some companies place a ceiling on the cost of a single hospital stay, while most cap the amount you can be paid in your lifetime. Usually these caps are set quite high, such as $1 million over a lifetime, but you should find out at what point your insurance company will no longer cover your bills.

Hospital Expenses. Your insurance company will also pay some charges from the hospital itself, such as room, board, and medications, based on a preset fee schedule. Insurers often pay the costs of doctors, surgeons, and other specialists who serve you while you're a patient in the hospital. If you are hospitalized away from your hometown, your charges may also be covered by your insurance company, although it may pay only up to the amount it would pay for the same procedures in your hometown.

Catastrophic Claims. In addition to your basic health coverage, most employers provide major medical insurance, which is designed to protect against catastrophic claims. This type of insurance sometimes covers procedures that basic plans do not, or it might set higher limits for the same services. Major medical plans usually pay for hospital care, intensive nursing care, prescription drugs you take at home, and special medical equipment or devices. Like regular medical coverage, however, major medical plans also impose deductibles and coinsurance requirements.

Dental and Vision Care. Most medical plans do not cover these categories of health care. They are usually provided as separate plans, with their own premiums, deductibles, and co-payments. The amount of coverage can vary significantly, allowing only a certain number of cleanings, X-rays, or vision tests each year.

Discount Prescription Drug Plans. This option is another increasingly popular benefit. To cut down on the cost of drugs purchased by employees, companies enroll in drug plans offered by commercial insurance companies, labor unions, HMOs, and mail-order drug services. Some employers pay the entire cost of these plans, while others require workers to contribute at least part of the cost through regular payroll deduction. If you have a chronic illness (such as asthma) that requires regular medication, or if you have children, then a prescription drug plan can save you money. But if you are young, healthy, and have no family responsibilities, you may not need such a plan.

Estimating Your Medical Expenses: The Cost of the Trip

All of these health benefits can add up in terms of the money you can save, if you obtain coverage from your employer so you don't have to pay out of your own pocket for your medical, hospital, dental, and eye care expenses. One way to get a better financial handle on what your expenses might be is to calculate your medical costs for each of the past few years, including

- ▶ visits to your doctor for regular checkups (the younger you are, the less often you need a regular checkup)
- ▶ visits to your dentist or hygienist for regular cleanings (twice a year if your teeth are in good condition)
- ▶ prescription drugs you take regularly

Dependent Care Benefits: Discount Packages

In addition to flexible spending accounts (FSAs) for reimbursement of child or elder care, many companies offer other valuable dependent care benefits that can save you money. The following are just two of the innovative programs that some employers sponsor. Even though these options may not be relevant to you when you're starting out, they're something to keep in mind for later on down the road:

1. *Companies sometimes offer child care centers at or near your place of employment.* These centers can be run either by your company or by a day care firm that specializes in operating such centers. Because they are expensive to run, they are usually not free. However, you might pay rates that are lower than those of a commercial day care center, which can be a significant savings. Some employers, rather than supporting a child care center of their own, contribute to a community center that reserves places for their employees' children.

2. *Adoption assistance is also becoming increasingly available from many companies.* Some firms donate cash of up to $2,000 to help cover the myriad costs of adopting a child. Others grant paid or unpaid leave for generally up to 6 or 12 weeks.

Flexible Spending Accounts (FSAs): Extra Insurance

Despite rising health insurance costs, some companies offer at least one bit of good news in the form of *flexible spending accounts* (FSAs). If your firm offers an FSA, you can pay the ever-increasing insurance premiums, deductibles, and co-payments, as well as drugstore items, etc., with pretax dollars instead of expensive after-tax dollars. In addition, you can use the FSA to pay for dependent and child care expenses, which may not matter to you now when you're just starting out, but it's certainly something to consider down the road if you're planning to have kids.

A typical FSA works as follows: At the beginning of each year, you tell your company how much you want to set aside to fund the FSA for that year (up to $5,000). That amount is then deducted off the top of your paycheck and invested in an FSA. This is another toll-free road on which you don't have to pay federal, state, local, or Social Security taxes. In some cases your employer will also contribute to your FSA.

Over the next year you incur medical expenses, including deductibles, co-payments, and premiums, that are not fully covered by your health insurance. In addition, you might have medical expenses that are never covered by your insurance, such as elective surgery or cosmetic dental work. All of these costs can be paid for with the money you set aside in your FSA. Later on you might pay child care expenses or the costs of having a parent live with you, which are both covered by FSAs.

Be careful when you determine how much money to invest in an FSA because they usually are a "use it or lose it" proposition. If you do not claim the money in the FSA by the end of the year, you forfeit it forever. Therefore, use the amount you paid out of pocket last year as a guide to figuring the coming year's FSA contribution. Be a bit conservative in estimating how much of your medical expenses will not be covered by your regular health insurance. It's better to end the year having too many unreimbursed expenses to submit to your FSA than too few. The worksheet in Tollbooth 3.3 will help you determine how much to set aside in your health care FSA. Remember, you receive only one opportunity a year to set the amount, unless a major change occurs in your personal situation, such as a marriage or the birth of a child.

If your company offers an FSA, and you have unreimbursed medical and dependent care expenses, sign up for the plan. The example in Tollbooth 3.4 illustrates how much money you could save by funding an FSA. The example assumes you are single with no children, report $45,000 a year in earnings, and deposit $1,000 in a health FSA. The following Web site has a calculator that will help you select the right amount to deposit in your FSA: https://www.fsafeds.com/fsafeds/fsa_calculator.asp.

Tollbooth 3.3

FSA Funding Worksheet

	$ Amount
Annual Deductible for Medical Plan	_____
Annual Deductible for Dental Plan	_____
Co-payment for Medical Plan (the portion of expenses not covered)	_____
Co-payment for Dental Plan	_____
Elective Surgery (cosmetic surgery, laser eye surgery, major dental bills)	_____
Hearing Care (testing and hearing aids)	_____
Orthodontia	_____
Psychotherapy (the portion of expenses not covered by your medical plan)	_____
Routine Physical Exams	_____
Vision Care (testing and eyeglasses)	_____
Total unreimbursed medical expenses	_____

The example in Tollbooth 3.4 calculates only the federal income taxes you would save. In fact, you would also sidestep state and local taxes. (More toll-free roads!) If your state and local taxes are high, the difference can add up. If your company does not yet offer one, talk to your benefits officer, your boss, or anyone you know who is in upper management. Such plans are usually adopted when employees clamor for them.

Employee Assistance Programs (EAPs): For Bumps in the Road

An increasingly common benefit that many companies provide besides health and dependent care plans is the *employee assistance program* (EAP). Such confidential plans are designed to help employees cope with the many stresses and strains of modern life. Some of the areas EAPs cover include help for the following problems:

Tollbooth 3.4

Amount Saved by Funding an FSA

	Using the FSA	Not Using the FSA
Income	$45,000	$45,000
Minus FSA Deposits	– 1,000	– 0
Taxable Income	44,000	45,000
Minus Federal Taxes (28 percent Tax bracket)	– 7,731	– 7,994
Take-Home Pay	36,269	37,006
Minus After-Tax Expenses	– 0	– 1,000
Spendable Pay	36,269	36,006
Tax Savings ("Using the FSA") minus not ("Using the FSA")	$ 263	$ 0

▶ *Drug, alcohol, or other substance abuse.* This type of assistance can save not only your job or your career but also your life. The cost of residential treatment for addiction can run into thousands of dollars for a week's stay, and the cost of not getting treatment can be job loss and irreparable damage to one's career.

▶ *Mental health and emotional issues.* EAPs often offer counseling from psychologists that can be helpful after a death in the family or the breakup of a relationship. Both events can affect your job performance, which may reduce your chance of a promotion and raises, so don't dismiss the EAP as lacking monetary value.

▶ *Disabilities affecting you or a family member.* EAP counselors can help you find specialized care providers to help you or your loved one overcome a disability and function effectively and efficiently on the job and at home.

▶ *Marital and family problems.* EAPs often offer sessions with marriage counselors and provide help with the stresses of finding good child care or dealing with an elderly parent whose health is failing. Marriage or couples counseling with a qualified psychologist can range from $60 to more than $150 in urban areas.

▶ *Financial problems caused by excessive debt or spending sprees.* EAP counselors are usually not financial planners, but they may provide financial or debt counseling and they can refer you to appropriate experts.

▶ *Legal problems.* EAP counselors are not lawyers, but they can help determine whether you need a lawyer and, if so, how to find a good one.

Employers who offer such progressive EAPs realize that a normally productive employee can be dragged down by any one of these problems, and that it is cost-effective to offer help in a time of turmoil. If your employer is one of the enlightened few, take advantage of the services if you need them.

Company-Sponsored Life Insurance Programs: "Collision" Insurance

Most companies offer several forms of insurance protection to their employees. When you're just starting out, life insurance and its cost may not be important to you, but if you're married, have children, or are thinking about starting a family, this benefit becomes more important. Companies buy coverage at group rates that are significantly less expensive than you could buy on your own. Most employers provide minimal life insurance for their active employees at little or no cost. This coverage is designed to help the survivors of deceased employees cope with the potentially devastating loss of income that can occur when someone dies.

Term Life Insurance

Many companies offer group life insurance, usually at a much lower price than you can obtain by purchasing individual life insurance. Most companies buy *term insurance,* which is payable only if an employee dies. Unlike whole or variable life insurance, term insurance provides no cash value buildup or savings component. Term contracts usually run for a year at a time, at which point they are normally renewed, which is why these policies are called *annual renewable term.*

The amount of term insurance provided for each employee varies. It is usually calculated as a percentage of the worker's salary, up to twice his or her annual gross pay. Therefore, a worker making $30,000 a year would be insured for $60,000. Other companies cover all employees for the same dollar amount, such as $50,000, no matter what the salary.

In the vast majority of cases, employers pick up the entire cost of the insurance premiums. When employees must chip in, they pay a flat amount per month, based on a formula. For example, you might pay $.15 per $1,000 of coverage. If you're covered for $50,000, you would have to pay $7.50 a month, or $90 a year. According to IRS regulations, the premium on any group life insurance benefit up to $50,000 is not considered taxable income. On any benefit exceeding $50,000, which is called *supplemental coverage,* the excess premium is considered taxable income and will be reported on your W-2. Usually companies require that you contribute some or all of the premiums on coverage of more than $50,000.

▶ Disability Insurance: When the Car Breaks Down

If you have a serious illness or accident or are otherwise injured while not on the job, your medical bills will probably be covered by your employer's disability income insurance plan if you have one. Unlike workers' compensation plans (often known as workers' comp) that pay only if you are injured on the job, disability programs pay a regular income if you have a prolonged illness or injury that occurred off the job. Workers' comp is a program run by your state labor department to cover medical costs and to replace lost wages. Disability coverage is private insurance designed to pay for short-term and long-term illnesses and injuries.

You can qualify for two kinds of disability payment plans if you are sick or injured and unable to work. Short-term plans sometimes replace your income for up to a year (52 weeks), although half a year (26 weeks) is more common. You qualify for short-term disability if your illness or injury makes it impossible for you to perform your normal job functions. Before you begin collecting disability, however, you must prove that your disability is serious. Once you do so, you must wait at least a week for your first check. For that week or so, you may receive your full salary according to your company's sick leave policy. Once the disability checks start, you can count on getting up to about two-thirds (67 percent) of your salary, which is fully taxable ordinary income. Not all employers offer short-term disability insurance to their employees.

If you are still not able to work after 26 to 52 weeks of short-term disability, you may transfer to long-term disability coverage, which is offered by more, but not all, employers. To qualify, you must be incapable of performing not only your prior job but also any other job that you are reasonably suited for—just about any job you *can* do. Long-term disability payments, when combined with Social Security disability payments, can amount to as much as 80 percent of your former salary. However, it is extremely difficult to qualify for Social Security disability even if you qualify for your employer's group plan. Most long-term disability plans will pay the agreed upon amount for a specific number of years (usually at least 10) or until you reach age 65, when Social Security and your employer's pension plan (if you have one) kick in.

Although the costs of short-term disability plans are usually paid completely by employers, the costs of long-term disability plans are typically shared by employers and employees. An LTD line on your paycheck stub indicates how much you pay toward long-term disability insurance premiums.

Most employees pay little attention to disability insurance coverage until they have an accident or suffer some other disabling misfortune and need the insurance money to survive. If you are offered a chance to buy long-term disability coverage through your employer, grab it. Such coverage can be relatively inexpensive (under $100 per month for a healthy, young single person). If you ever need it, the plan could be an enormous help in getting you through a difficult time. Disability coverage is one type of insurance that you should not skimp on!

The whole field of employee benefits can be complex and confusing. As you can see, it is extremely worthwhile to delve into the information on employee benefits packages when you start work at a new company. By taking full advantage of your employer's retirement, health, dependent care, employee assistance, education, legal, and insurance programs, you will be better able to improve your financial well-being and realize your financial goals than if you ignore or don't bother to understand the benefits information that your company provides.

▶ Put Your Pedal to the Metal: Getting Ahead

There are many benefits of moving to a new job, especially if it's higher up on the career ladder, although even a lateral move to another company or another type of work can bring rewards. But before you drive away from your current situation, consider all the financial factors. Consider the cost and the quality of plans. Tally up all your income: your salary, bonuses, options, 401(k) plan, benefits, and tuition reimbursement. When considering another job offer, you need to remember to compare all of these factors, not just your salary.

Learn the Language

Key Terms to Know about Employee Benefits

401(k) A defined contribution plan that allows employees of a corporation to have tax-deferred retirement savings. It is named after the paragraph in the IRS tax code that describes it.

403(b) A defined contribution plan that allows employees of a nonprofit organization, such as a school, hospital, church, or social welfare agency, to have tax-deferred retirement savings. It is named after the paragraph in the IRS tax code that describes it.

annuity A lifelong income stream. In the context of this chapter, an annuity is a type of financial vehicle in which employees can receive their retirement benefits once they retire. Employees receive a specific monthly sum for a particular period of time (in contrast to receiving a lump-sum payment upon retirement).

COBRA The Consolidated Omnibus Budget Reconciliation Act, passed in 1985, that requires employers (in most cases) to provide continued group insurance to employees, often for 18 months after the employee leaves the company (though small companies often offer COBRA for 6 months). The employee, however, pays full premiums plus administrative costs.

defined benefit plan A type of company retirement plan, usually offered in the form of a pension plan, in which the company promises to provide a specified retirement benefit.

defined contribution plan A type of company retirement plan in which the company promises to make certain contributions, and in which employees are often allowed to make contributions to the plan, sometimes on a pretax basis. Examples include employee stock ownership plans, money purchase pension plans, profit-sharing plans, 401(k) or 403(b) plans, stock bonus plans, and thrift plans.

EAP Employee Assistance Program. A benefit offered by many companies as an extension of health benefits. The EAP is a confidential counseling service to help employees with mental health and emotional issues, substance abuse problems, family or marital problems, and financial, legal, or other problems that are causing stress.

ESOP Employee Stock Ownership Plan. This benefit allows employees to share in the profits of their company. Employee and company contributions are invested in company stock, which gives employees more incentive to work diligently and help the company prosper.

FSA Flexible Spending Account. A health care option in which employees can set aside pretax dollars for the coming year instead of expensive after-tax dollars to pay for anticipated medical or other expenses, such as child care or elder care.

HMO Health Maintenance Organization. One of several health insurance options offered by employers. In most HMOs, the services provided by a doctor or another health care professional are paid in whole or in part either directly to the provider or are reimbursed to employees by an insurance company.

IRA Individual Retirement Account. This savings vehicle was originally used by self-employed individuals who didn't have the benefit of a company retirement or pension plan, though today it is used in addition to corporate plans.

Keogh A type of retirement plan that allows entrepreneurs to set aside money for retirement in the same manner as employees of large corporations.

pension The traditional type of corporate retirement benefit plan, in which the employer sets aside and invests a certain amount of money in a trust fund for each employee every year. Upon retirement, the plan pays employees a monthly pension benefit, normally based on how long the employees have worked at the firm and the salary level that they attained at the time of retirement.

PPO Preferred Provider Organization. This health care option is a type of health insurance coverage featuring a network of affiliated doctors, hospitals, and other health care operations that offer medical services to a large group of employees at predetermined rates. Employees using a PPO can visit any doctor they want and providers are generally paid directly for that visit by the health insurance company.

SEP Simplified Employee Pension Plan. This savings vehicle is a simpler, small-company version of the defined-contribution plan offered by larger employers.

SIMPLE Savings Incentive Match Plan for Employees, also known as SIM-PLE IRAs. These plans are similar to 401(k) plans but are for companies with fewer than 100 employees earning at least $5,000 a year. If a company offers the SIMPLE plan, it cannot offer other qualified retirement plans to its workers.

Vesting The accumulation of years of service in a company that gives the employee the legal right to receive some or all of the company's available benefits upon reaching retirement age, even if that employee no longer works for that employer. The number of years varies depending on the plan.

Moving on Down the Road

Renting an Apartment vs. Buying a House

Chapters 1–3 focused primarily on helping you manage your money and explaining ways that you can increase the amount available to you, by using credit carefully and maximizing the benefits available from your employer. This chapter helps you spend your money wisely, beginning with one of the biggest decisions you'll face when starting out on your own: determining whether you will buy or rent your home and how you will pay for it.

▶ Different Roads, Different Tolls: Deciding Whether to Rent or Buy

If you're just starting out in life, you're probably either living at home with your parents or other family members, or you're living in a dorm room, ready to leave college and move into your own place. The first financial question you need to ask is: Can I afford to move out? If so, can you go it alone, or will you need one or more roommates or housemates? Finally, you need to determine what you can afford. Are you ready to buy a house (or condo or co-op), or would it be better to rent an apartment for a while? The answer requires not only that you make financial decisions, but that you also make lifestyle choices that will affect your financial life, which we'll also discuss in this chapter.

Most people just starting out will rent an apartment, because most of us don't have the money to buy a home right off the bat or because we are not ready to make that level of commitment yet. According to a recent National Association of Home Builders survey, 70 percent of tenants regard the cost of rent as the first consideration when looking for an apartment; location is the second consideration; and security, neighborhood, and community assets follow.

Unfortunately, many renters do not have this luxury. Rents nationwide are high, and many people are paying more than the government-recommended limit of 30 percent of their income on rent. For this reason some people decide to stay in their family's home until they've saved enough money for a down payment on a house. And many parents often help out by making a low-interest loan (or, even better, a no-interest loan!) to their kids for this purpose.

Choosing a Direction: Calculating What You Can Afford

Whether you decide to rent or buy, you need to review your financial situation and determine how much you can afford on a monthly basis. Another factor that will play into this calculation is deciding how long you plan to stay in your next home. If you're not sure you're going to stay in the same state, city, or neighborhood (downtown vs. the suburbs), you might want to rent for a few years until you settle somewhere. Many people just starting out relocate to other cities, either for a new job, a new industry, or a new relationship. Buying a house and then selling it in less than three years or so later is probably not worthwhile financially, unless you expect to sell it for much more than you paid, and if you don't mind the time spent finding and closing on a house and then reselling it soon afterward, paying realtors' commissions of 6 or 7 percent.

If you decide to rent, you need to consider not only the *net* rent, which is the monthly cost you'll pay your landlord, but you also need to calculate your *gross* rent, which consists of gas, hot water, and electricity, if they aren't included in your rent. In some cases your landlord may also charge you for parking, storage, and security services. You may also have to pay a surcharge for use of the deck, playroom, pool, game room, and laundry room, if you

Dear Jeanine,

I bought a house! And thanks to Mom for letting me live at home since I graduated, I can afford it! It was so great of her to ask me to pay only grocery bills instead of board. I saved so much of my income in only two years. I didn't want to get an apartment and pay rent; it's time to get my own place, to build some equity, and have the tax advantages of a mortgage.

It's a row home, which is perfect for a single woman, and it's not too far from Mom, though she still has Jack living with her for at least a few more years. You're lucky you're married with a nice house in the 'burbs, but that might happen for me, too. Tom and I are getting serious, and he likes the new house, so we think we'll live here until we can afford something bigger. We both want kids, and with two incomes, a bigger house should be easily affordable. But this is a great starter house.

You'll have to come visit the next time you're in town! Gotta run: Mom and I are going shopping for furniture.

Love,

Christina

have any or all of these, though they are extras that are not charged for the typical apartment.

If you decide to buy, don't make the mistake of thinking that your only housing expense will be your mortgage payment. Homeowners face costs that renters do not. You'll need to pay for the following:

- ▶ mortgage (more about this soon)
- ▶ taxes (real estate)
- ▶ insurance
- ▶ maintenance (lawn care, snow removal, roof repair, hot water heater)

▶ homeowners' fees for a condo, co-op, or association
▶ all utilities

Now that you know what the basic expenses will be, consider your specific financial situation. Let's make a quick U-turn and review the financial information you compiled in Chapter 1 when you created your budget, especially Roadmaps 1.2, 1.3, and 1.4, which listed your expenses. Once you've done that, we can build on these maps and provide a clearer estimate. Tollbooth 4.1 provides an easy way to calculate how much you'll be able to pay.

If You Rent, Should You Travel Alone? Or Find Someone to "Share the Driving"?

You might have noticed that Tollbooth 4.1 includes entries for four lease signers; namely, roommates or housemates. Obviously, it's easier to afford an apartment if there's more than one of you paying for it. Many people just starting out decide to combine their incomes and find a larger apartment or even a house to rent. Before you decide to go down that road, though, let's pull over and consider some of the implications of such a decision. Because this is a personal finance book, we'll focus on the financial implications, though you should also consider whether your personality and lifestyle will be compatible with the roommates you're considering.

Establishing Rules of the Road: Who Pays for What?

From the beginning, you and your roommate should have fundamental agreements. Ask yourselves what is the maximum amount that each of you is willing and able to spend for gross rent? How will you divide the rent if the space allocated to each roommate differs? And how will you decide who gets the larger space? It's probably one of the first discussions you'll have with a prospective roommate.

Communication and responsibility may be the key words when it comes to living with a roommate. Having a roommate also involves courtesy and mutual respect as well as the necessity of dealing with money issues. A successful roommate situation is one in which everyone knows what to expect and respects the arrangements. The following suggestions may make your roommate experience more successful:

1. Pay your share of the rent on time to one designated person.
2. Make sure the designated person pays the rent on time and gets a receipt.

Tollbooth 4.1

How Much Rent Can You Afford?

Ability to Pay

Monthly gross income (earnings, interest, other)
Lease signer #1 $ _____
Lease signer #2 (a roommate)   _____
Lease signer #3   _____
Lease signer #4   _____
Total Income   _____

Affordability Test #1

Total income $_____ × 30 percent (.30) = $ _____
[Most landlords require that your rent equal no more than
30 percent of your gross income to qualify.]

Recurring Obligations

Car loans $ _____
Student loans   _____
Other loans   _____
Tuition   _____
Memberships and dues   _____
Alimony, maintenance, child support   _____
Medical insurance and payments   _____
Car insurance (prorated monthly)   _____
Other recurring expenditures   _____
Payroll taxes   _____

Other Monthly Expenses

Monthly credit card payments $ _____
Food   _____
Charitable contributions   _____
Entertainment   _____
Insurance (all other types)   _____
Clothing (other than credit card charges)   _____
Travel (other than charges)   _____
Vehicle expenses and repairs   _____
Local transportation and parking   _____
Work-related costs (lunches, etc.)   _____
Laundry and dry cleaning   _____
Savings and investments   _____
Textbooks and school supplies   _____

Other monthly expenses	
Total Monthly Obligations	

Affordability Test #2

Subtract total monthly income from total monthly obligations to determine what is left for the gross rent.

Total monthly income	$ _____
Total monthly obligations	− _____
Maximum Available for Gross Rent	= _____

3. Agree on a formula for sharing utility bills that reflect each roommate's usage. Separate window air conditioners can lead to difficulty because they consume a lot of power that roommates without air conditioners may pay for, unless a special formula for paying the electric bill is arranged.

4. Put all recurring bills, such as utilities and cable TV, in everyone's names. If that's not possible, then each roommate might want to obtain responsibility for one of the utility services. It might require a powwow once a month to reconcile the accounts. If each person is fully at risk for his or her bill, each will respect the risks of the others and be more likely to pay up.

5. Encourage your roommates to have their own phones to avoid problems with the phone bill and opt to have no house phone. If you decide to share one phone line, watch out for hazards.

6. Agree on how you will manage the cable TV decisions. Who will pay what portion of the cable bill? What will you decide about the pay-for-play features? How will you control that and allocate it to the right persons? Will only one person have the authorization code?

7. Negotiate how you will handle food issues. If you decide to share food, how will the cost get divvied up? Who will buy for the group? Who will choose the basics for inclusion? If you opt not to share food, how will you keep it separate? How will you handle the inevitable notes that say, "I drank the last of Bill's milk and owe him a quart"?

8. Determine how you will deal with household supplies, such as cleaning expenses, toilet paper, paper towels, and the like. If you share, will the cost be divided? Who will shop for the supplies? Will the shopping tasks be rotated? Where will the receipts go?

Hazard!

Costs to consider if you and your roommates share a phone line:

► Who pays for long distance?
► How about local calls?
► Do you have call waiting? What is the etiquette of it? Does the person on the phone take a message or relinquish the phone?
► How will you handle a situation in which one roommate is online for hours tying up the phone?
► What about 976 and 900 calls? Will you have the phone company block these numbers?
► If each roommate pays for his or her calls, who divvies up the phone bill each month?

9. Decide who will clean your place. Labor sometimes is the same as cash. Are you going to hire a cleaning service, or are these chores going to be shared? Who will be in charge of making a schedule and checking on the work? Of course, you can't wait for a maid to do the dishes or remove hair from the drain. Will people accept certain personal tasks between cleanings?

Another area of financial responsibility is renters' insurance. It's a good idea for roommates, as a group, to acquire this type of insurance. This protection can help you handle not only problems with theft and water leaks, but will also help you deal with issues of liability; for example, if you or your roommates have a party, and someone is hurt while on the premises. Renters' insurance typically runs only a couple of hundred dollars a year (about $20 per month). When you split it with several roommates, the cost is negligible and the benefits are invaluable.

As you can see, some of these financial decisions will become lifestyle discussions, but let's stay on course with the financial focus. Make sure you discuss with your prospective roommates what each of you can afford and what each of you is willing to pay for. Finally, discuss how you and your roommates will handle the rent and other financial obligations if, for example, one of you loses your job. Contingency planning is worth considering.

"License and Registration, Please": Whose Name is on the Lease?

If you've agreed on all the preliminary financial considerations of having a roommate, and you've found a place you can all live with and afford, then all roommates should sign the lease (if it's a new lease) or have the lease modified to add new roommates. Most leases require the disclosure of additional people living in the rental unit and require that the landlord approve the additions. Adding others to the lease and having them acknowledged by the landlord is a good thing to do because it may protect everybody from being evicted for a breach of the lease, and they won't wreck the place because now they are also liable.

Some landlords will agree to collect the rent separately from each tenant, and some go so far as issuing separate leases, but this is extremely rare. This latter policy can get confusing when a tenant moves out or stops paying the rent because, ultimately, even though all residents are responsible for the full rent, they may live in the blissful belief that they are safe from eviction, which may not be true. In addition, having multiple leases active at the same time for the same premises can make for a legal mess when a lease cancellation or eviction looms on the horizon. Utility companies often use leases to determine who should pay the bill in cases of default of payment. So it's better to have one lease and one monthly lease payment so that everybody knows what's happening. When a roommate moves out, the name should be removed from the lease. (There are other issues pertaining to what to do when a roommate moves out, but that's too far down the road for us to consider at this point.)

Keep in mind that every person is "severally and jointly" responsible for the rent, damages, and other lease obligations, which means that each person can be sued separately for the full amount of the rent if the rent is not paid. Leases are binding contracts in this regard.

You should also consider how you will handle the situation when a roommate decides to leave, and you have a written lease lasting more than 30 days. Have a co-habitation agreement drawn up. You still need to pay the rent, even if your roommate moves out! Again, this is a little ways down the road, but it's worth considering and discussing with your roommate(s) before you move in. One way to handle this situation is to ask the departing roommate to find his or her replacement, if the lease isn't up before the move. And whoever leaves remains responsible for the rent portion until you or your roommate can find a suitable replacement; that is, somebody who is more or less like the departing roommate who will get along with the other roommates and pay the rent on time.

▶ Moving On Up: Should You Buy a Home?

Nearly 5 million people buy new and existing homes in the United States each year, and for many of them, it's their first home purchase. Almost two-thirds of this group are married, and most have spent between two and five years saving for a down payment. Most will buy a single-family home, with the remainder buying townhouses, condos, or co-ops.

The biggest reason people give for buying a home is that they are throwing money away paying rent. They contend that with a house payment they are at least building equity. For example, let's say that in 2003, you put down $20,000 on a $100,000 home, and you borrowed the remaining $80,000. Depending on where you lived, it would not have been unusual for your home to have appreciated about 10 percent over the next two years (from $100,000 to $110,000), thus making your equity $30,000 (the $20,000 you put down plus the $10,000 that your house's value has appreciated, excluding your net interest cost). That's a 50 percent increase—not bad.

But now let's say you bought a home in California in the early 1990s, a time when values dropped by as much as 20 percent, and the value stayed down for several years. (I know, you may have been only 10 years old in the early 1990s, but bear with me for the purposes of this example.) By the mid-1990s, your $100,000 home was worth only $80,000. Your equity was gone.

The pro-renter argument is just as faulty, however, and the numbers can be manipulated to say anything you want them to. For instance, let's say that instead of putting that $20,000 down on a house, you decided to rent and put that money in the stock market. Okay, let's imagine that in 1999, you took your $20,000 and bought stock in a company called Homestore.com, which is a Web site and technology company that advertises millions of old and new homes for sale nationwide. If you bought that stock at around $20 per share, within a few months you would have seen it bounce up to over $100 per share. Hooray! You turned your $20,000 investment into more than $100,000! (If you were clever enough to sell when the stock was at its peak.) If you continued to hold on to your Homestore.com stock for a couple of years, however, you would have seen the price of your stock dwindle to somewhere between $1 and $3. Your $20,000 investment would now be worth $1,000 to $3,000.

The point is that you cannot guarantee that stocks will go up, nor can you guarantee that home prices will go up. In addition, none of the numbers above factor in the significant costs inherent in home ownership, such as insurance, repairs, and maintenance costs. Nor do these numbers reflect rent increases, the cost of parking, lost security deposits because of damage to the rental unit, and so forth.

Be very careful about using the electronic calculators you find on the Internet—and there are hundreds of them out there. There really isn't a calculator that does a good job of factoring in every financial variable. For example, what if you were to take your down payment money and invest it in Microsoft instead. Would you be ahead or behind?

Quite frankly, most of the calculators produce outcomes that the Web site wants them to produce. Real estate company/industry calculators almost always tip toward home ownership. In contrast, apartment Web sites tend to favor renting. (Go to the "rent versus own" section of http://www.NMHC.org, operated by the National Multi Housing Council.) Banking sites also tend to favor home ownership, because the bank wants to sell the mortgage.

Cut to the Chase: Can You Afford to Buy a Home?

You're probably going to be better off financially owning rather than renting a home over the long term, but it's not a slam dunk. And you may not be able to afford your own home. So let's see whether you can or not.

Tollbooth 4.1 helped you calculate what you can afford in terms of gross rent. Let's take that number and see how it compares to a mortgage. (See Tollbooth 4.2.)

But you need to know more than how a mortgage will compare to rent, though. There are four basic financial questions you must answer to decide whether you can afford to buy a home:

1. How much money can you afford to pay for a home?
2. How big a monthly payment can you afford?
3. How much money will you need to pay for the down payment?
4. How much do you anticipate for annual repairs and maintenance?

These are all questions that you will need to answer before you can realistically go house hunting. It's a waste of time, effort, and hope to look at

Tollbooth 4.2

Can You Afford to Buy? Monthly Rent vs. a Mortgage Payment

The following formula arbitrarily assumes that 10 percent of your mythical mortgage payment will cover homeowners insurance and the repayment of the principal, with the rest paying deductible interest and property taxes. It also assumes that your top tax bracket (known to accountants as your *marginal tax rate*) is 28 percent. If your tax bracket is higher, your tax savings will be correspondingly higher.

A.	Your present rent	$_____
B.	Multiply by 1.32	× 1.32
C.	Equivalent monthly mortgage payment	$_____

The result (line C) is a rough estimate of the amount you can spend on a monthly mortgage payment, including the principal, interest, property taxes, and homeowners insurance, without owing any more money at the end of the income tax year than you would have by renting.

---

homes in the $300,000 to $375,000 range when you can only afford $175,000 to $250,000. It's important to know what you can afford before you invest too much shoe leather, miles per gallon, and day dreaming about finding the perfect home.

Don't Travel without a Tool Kit: Getting Preapproval for a Mortgage

In the past accurate information about purchasing a home was often difficult to come by. A real estate agent might tell you one thing, a seller might tell you something else, and a friend who seemed to know something about real estate might have another answer altogether. Fortunately, now you can quickly, easily, and, what is most important, accurately answer your financial home-buying questions. And in the process, you can acquire a tool that might allow you to leverage a better price. The tool is called "preapproval."

To get preapproved, you go through the process of applying for a mortgage from an actual lender before you've found a home. You fill out an application and put up a fee (usually under $50) for a credit report.

The lender looks at your application and your net worth statement and determines how much money you have for a down payment, what your income is, and how solid your credit history looks. From that information, the lender decides the maximum loan you can get, which tells you how much house you can buy (unless you can add money you've stashed under the mattress, or you've made a killing in the stock market, or you're getting help with the down payment from your family). After the underwriters approve, you get a letter stating that you are preapproved for the loan.

This is no time to be shy or embarrassed about finances; everything will come out sooner or later. It's better to be fully informed up front before you waste a lot of time looking at something unobtainable. Lenders use a formula to determine what percentage of your income you can afford to allocate toward purchasing a home. They also take a close look at your credit rating, which is why it's so important to take care of your credit. It's not something you can build or rebuild overnight.

Certainly, the more you earn and the more you have in savings or assets, the better financial picture you can paint. Regardless of what you think your situation may be, it's important to know with certainty whether you can afford to buy a home. Get preapproval to make sure you're not overreaching.

Your preapproval letter may state that you can borrow up to a certain amount of money at a specific interest rate. Or it may state that you are preapproved for a maximum monthly payment. Lenders prefer to name a maximum monthly payment. The reason is that although the most you can afford to pay monthly won't change, interest rates will. As interest rates go up, your maximum loan amount will go down. As interest rates go down, your maximum loan amount will go up.

The preapproval letter is something both you and a home seller can bank on, literally. It is a commitment from a lender to loan you money. The letter says that if the property you wish to buy is of an appropriate value, and if your financial situation doesn't change, you will get financing. The lender stands behind you.

In short, preapproval will tell you

▶ your maximum monthly payment,
▶ your maximum loan,
▶ your minimum down payment.

The preapproval letter will also tell you that you are virtually guaranteed a loan. With your preapproval completed, you will know how much you can afford to pay for a home.

Detour: Another Advantage of Preapproval

A preapproval letter can be heavy artillery that will motivate sellers. Consider the position of the sellers. They want a good price for their home, but they also know that most buyers must get a mortgage in order to purchase. This situation introduces uncertainty. Will the buyers be able to get a mortgage large enough to make the purchase? In the past, this step was a gamble, and even today the uncertainty remains for many buyers. The sellers won't know whether the sale can be completed until they have signed a sales agreement, and the buyers have spent a few weeks trying to find a mortgage.

On the other hand, when the buyers are preapproved, it's a sure thing. They've already been to a lender. The lender has already said yes. What's there to be uncertain about? When you're competing against buyers who don't have preapproval, you're the one most likely to win the deal, all else being equal. And when you're offering a lower price than the seller is asking, you might be more likely to get your offer accepted, all because you have preapproval.

Getting a preapproval letter is the best way to determine how big a mortgage and how big a house you can afford. And it's also a good way to get a better deal.

A Better Road: Preapproval for a Mortgage Beats Prequalified

On your journey toward getting preapproved, you may hear someone speak of getting you "prequalified" (or simply "qualified"). Listen carefully. Don't be misled. Prequalification is nothing more than receiving a statement of opinion. The opinion can be given by anyone and simply states that you are likely to get a mortgage for a certain amount.

In the past real estate agents frequently prequalified their buyers with an oral statement of their financial worthiness. In truth, however, a prequalification is little more than an opinion, and no one stands behind it. As far as savvy buyers and sellers are concerned, it's of little value. Being prequalified says little more than maybe the buyers will get the mortgage, and then again maybe they won't.

While in many cases a prequalification letter is worth little more than the paper it's written on, it may not be totally worthless. Sometimes such a

What to Pack

Here's the information you need to provide to get preapproved for a mortgage:

▶ Recent paycheck stub
▶ Two years of income tax forms if you're self-employed
▶ Verification of deposit from your bank showing that you have the necessary down payment on account. The lender will likely have to sign the document and send it out directly. Sometimes your bankbook alone will do.
▶ Verification of employment from your employer showing how long you've been employed and stating your chances for continued employment. The lender will likely have to sign the document and will send it to your employer directly. Some lenders verify employment with just a phone call.
▶ Appraisal of property. This is not ordered by the lender until you return with a signed purchase agreement. You will have to pay for the appraisal.
▶ Proof of insurance on the property. You must obtain this from an insurance company. It will not be due until the deal is ready to close.
▶ Any other documents the lender may need, such as proof that you've paid off an old loan that shows up unpaid in a credit report.

letter indicates that someone checked your financial information and ran a credit report on you. But unfortunately, that someone wasn't a lender who was willing to commit to backing you.

A Long Road Ahead: Start the Preapproval Process Early

It's wise to start the preapproval process early because it can take some time to complete. The lender has to evaluate your application, secure a credit check, and perhaps verify your employment and savings (for your down payment). Then your application must be sent to underwriting where secondary lenders will check it over and give approval. Only then will the lender issue the preapproval letter. The process might take only a few days (if the lender does it electronically), or it might take a month or more if a problem is discovered that you must correct.

By the way, some lenders will offer you a preliminary preapproval letter. This means that they have taken your application and have completed a credit report, but they have not yet obtained underwriting approval. A preliminary preapproval letter will say that you're preapproved subject to underwriting. It's not as good as an actual preapproval letter, but it is easier to get, particularly if you're short on time.

Another good reason to start early getting your preapproval letter is that you may discover that there's a problem that will take time to resolve; for example, a credit check might show that you have unpaid bills, late payments, or even a bankruptcy. Although it's true that you should have been aware of these problems, we're only human, and sometimes we forget or choose to forget. If a problem crops up while you're getting preapproved, you usually have time to do something about it. If you wait until you're in the midst of a mortgage deal, the delay could cause you to lose the home you want most.

Or there could be an error at the credit bureau. Perhaps the bureau has mistaken you for someone else. Or it didn't receive word that a loan was paid off. Or a lender improperly stated that you hadn't paid when you had. In short, almost anything can go wrong, and until you check it out, you won't know. These examples give you good reason to check your own credit in advance of when you need it. As mentioned in Chapter 2, there are three national credit bureaus, and they also handle real estate financing: Equifax, Experian, and Trans Union (phone numbers and Web site addresses in Chapter 2). For a nominal fee, they will give you a report on your credit.

Problems other than credit sometimes crop up when you apply for a mortgage. You might not have enough income to warrant a mortgage as large as you want. Or perhaps in order to get a mortgage, you need to put 20 percent down instead of 10 percent. (On a $125,000 home, that's an extra $12,500 you'll have to come up with in cash!)

In short, the problems that can and often do arise can seem endless. And you won't know about them until you actually apply for the mortgage, which is one of the big reasons that sellers are so worried about buyers who don't have preapproval letters.

Directions, Please: Where to Go to Get Preapproval

Any legitimate lender can preapprove you. And remember, it should cost you nothing except the $50 or so for the credit report. If a lender wants to charge for preapproval, walk out. There are plenty of other lenders out there. Here are your choices, most of which can be found in the Yellow Pages:

- ▶ banks
- ▶ savings and loan associations
- ▶ mortgage brokers

- ▶ mortgage bankers
- ▶ credit unions

Banks offer mortgages, but they don't specialize in them. Banks spend more of their efforts on car loans and commercial finance. Mortgage brokers are the lenders of choice for most first-time homebuyers. Mortgage brokers are individuals or companies that work with major lenders, such as banks and insurance companies. These brokers provide the retail service that the more traditional lenders no longer offer. A good mortgage broker will offer a wide variety of mortgage types from dozens of different lenders. It's like shopping at a grocery store for potato chips rather than tracking down a Frito-Lay company outlet. All the brands are readily available. And you won't be paying more by dealing with a mortgage broker instead of a direct lender, such as a bank. Interest rates and fees are almost always comparable.

A mortgage banker is a lender of mortgages similar to a regular bank, but the mortgage banker has only one function: making real estate loans. Some of the country's largest independent lenders are mortgage bankers that deal directly with consumers.

The Internet is the up-and-coming lender of choice. Many mortgages now originate on the Internet, and within the next few years the vast majority of mortgages will originate there. The reasons for the growth of Internet mortgages are convenience and savings. Although you can get preapproved on the Internet and find some of the best financing available, you must choose your e-lender wisely. Some online lenders to check out include the following:

- ▶ LendingTree.com (http://www.lendingtree.com)
- ▶ E-Loan (http://www.eloan.com)
- ▶ JPMorgan Chase (http://www.chase.com)
- ▶ http://www.homefair.com

Touring a lender's Web site is an enlightening experience. Almost all of the loan sites will calculate your monthly payment if you simply input the principal, interest rate, and term of your mortgage. Most sites also include "wizards" that recommend the type of loan you should get based on your critical financial information. The mortgage calculators are usually excellent. However, most of the wizards leave a lot to be desired.

Getting preapproved online is more difficult. Only a few sites handle this. Essentially they require that you go through the same process that you would if you were applying for a mortgage, except that you won't list a property address. There is usually a fee for the credit check, although this may be refundable.

Using the Internet for preapproval is not only convenient, but it is also cheaper because there are discounts. Internet loans are not true retail mortgages. They are somewhere between retail (from a mortgage broker) and wholesale (from a direct lender, such as a bank). There is no storefront or secretarial staff, so the savings get passed on to you. The discount can sometimes be as much as 1 percent of the loan amount or more. In addition, some Internet lenders may offer to reimburse you for the costs of both the appraisal and the credit report if you follow through and get the mortgage from them.

But be careful. Not all lenders on the Internet are for real. It's very hard to judge whether you're dealing with a true mortgage company or some guy working out of his garage. You don't want to send intimate financial information to a fly-by-night operation that might use the information unscrupulously. If you don't recognize a lender's name as that of a legitimate company, check the lender with the Better Business Bureau and with banking officials in the lender's state. *Never send money or reveal any of your personal financial information until you know you're dealing with a legitimate lender.*

Electronic lending is definitely the wave of the future. For more information on getting a loan over the Internet, see Appendix B. Finally, Tollbooth 4.3 helps you determine the mortgage you may *qualify* for, not to be confused with what you may be able to *afford,* based on the formulas used by lenders and mortgage brokers.

▶ Saving for Your Trip: Budgeting for a Mortgage

Once you've been preapproved for a mortgage, you know how large a loan you can get. Finding a home is often a compromise between what you want and what you can afford. You've heard the expression "champagne taste on a beer budget." Housing is no different. Getting preapproved only tells you how much financing you can get. Now you need to decide how much you will feel comfortable spending. After all, you have to pay the bills. A good place to start is by looking again at the budget you created in Chapter 1.

First, look at your total monthly income and expenditures and see how much is left over for a house payment. Again, Roadmaps 1.2, 1.3, and 1.4 in Chapter 1 will help you tally your actual current expenses. Try to be candid: If you haven't already done this exercise, put down what you are actually spending, not what you wish you were spending.

Tollbooth 4.3

Calculating How Much House You Can Afford

Principal borrowed: $200,000.00

Annual payments: 12

Total payments: 360*

Annual interest rate: 6.00 percent

Periodic interest rate: 0.5000 percent

Regular mortgage payment amount: $1,199.10

Note: The following numbers are estimates. See an amortization schedule for more accurate values.

Total repaid: $431,676.00

Total interest paid: $231,676.00

Payment	Principal	Interest	Cum Prin	Cum Int	Prin Bal
1	199.10	1000.00	199.10	1000.00	199800.90
2	200.10	999.00	399.20	1999.00	199600.80
3	201.10	998.00	600.30	2997.00	199399.70
4	202.10	997.00	802.40	3994.00	199197.60
5	203.11	995.99	1005.51	4989.99	198994.49
6	204.13	994.97	1209.64	5984.96	198790.36
7	205.15	993.95	1414.79	6978.91	198585.21
8	206.17	992.93	1620.96	7971.84	198379.04
9	207.20	991.90	1828.16	8963.74	198171.84
10	208.24	990.86	2036.40	9954.60	197963.60

*only the first 10 payments of a typical 30-year mortgage are shown here.

Also, don't make the mistake of thinking that your only housing expense will be your mortgage payment. Homeowners face costs that renters do not. Use Tollbooth 4.4 to help you plan for these expenditures. Add these expenses to your previous total.

The amount left over from your income may now seem terribly small. This number is probably much smaller than the amount the lender says you can afford for a mortgage payment. If that's the case, it's time for compromise. Ask yourself what you might be willing to give up to own your first home.

Remember, buying a home is not like purchasing furniture or a car, nor is it like renting. Furniture and cars decline in value the moment they leave

Tollbooth 4.4

Calculating Additional Monthly Expenses if You Buy a Home

Property taxes and home insurance payments (if your lender hasn't already figured these costs into your preapproval mortgage payment)	$_____
Yard maintenance and landscaping	_____
Home repairs (buying a newer house helps here)	_____
Additional utilities (those that your landlord currently pays: gas, electric, water, garbage, sewage, and cable)	_____
Homeowners association dues	_____
Total monthly expenses less mortgage payment	_____

the showroom. And, as we've noted, some people believe that paying rent is like throwing money out the window each month. On the other hand, over time your home will likely increase in value. If each month it's worth more than it was the month before, you've got appreciation. And there are many other great advantages about home ownership to consider. Therefore, you may be willing to tighten your belt so you can pay more for a home of your own than you would be willing to spend on a rental. Think of your home purchase as an investment, as well as an expense, but don't go overboard and commit yourself to a payment that will sink you. Stretch yourself, but don't dream impossible dreams.

Additional Tolls: Taxes And Insurance

Sometimes when a lender preapproves a monthly mortgage payment, that figure includes property taxes as well as fire and homeowners insurance. It's called PITI in the lending trade: principal, interest (on the mortgage), taxes, and insurance.

But sometimes the preapproved monthly figure does not include taxes and insurance. If you put less than 20 percent down, the taxes and insurance are normally part of your monthly payment. If you put more than 20 percent down, taxes and insurance are paid separately if you choose. If you decide to pay taxes and insurance separately, be sure to include them as additional monthly expenses.

A useful rule of thumb for determining taxes and insurance is to calculate 2 percent of the likely value of the home if you live in a low-tax state, or 4–5 percent if you live in a high-tax state. Divide the result by 12 to find the monthly cost for taxes and insurance. Your real estate agent can tell you what the prior year's real estate taxes were and estimate what homeowner's insurance will cost.

One advantage is that all property taxes and interest on your mortgage (up to certain limits) are deductible from your income taxes. You can view the total amount of your tax savings as additional monthly income.

Here's how to calculate your tax savings. First, ask the lender what the total interest on your mortgage will be for the first full year. Next, ask your real estate agent what the taxes will be on the property. A good realtor should be able to give you a fairly accurate guess. Now add these two figures together to generate an estimate of your total deduction.

Calculating Your Mortgage Tax Deduction
$13,500 (interest) + 3,500 (taxes) = $17,000 (total deduction)

This is a large deduction. To determine how much this deduction will save you in taxes, first check with your accountant to see what your marginal tax bracket is. If you don't have an accountant, you can divide your year-to-date tax withholding by your year-to-date gross wages (from your paycheck stub), and this should give you a rough estimate of your tax bracket. If it happens to be 28 percent, here are your approximate savings:

Calculating Your Tax Savings
$17,000 (deductible amount) × 28 percent (tax bracket) = $4,760 (tax savings)

This is a great savings that will help balance out the high mortgage payments you might be struggling to pay. This is the good side of making the payments.

By making payments on your first home, you will save roughly $400 a month in federal taxes during the first year, which means you can have your employer reduce your federal tax withholding by $400 a month, thus increasing your take-home pay by a similar amount. Keep in mind that we're only considering federal income taxes at this point. If you pay state income taxes, you should also have savings on them. Again, don't forget to adjust for what you would have received had you taken only the standard deduction.

Hazard!

Remember, when calculating your tax savings on a mortgage, we're dealing with your marginal tax bracket. If your income decreases, you may fall back into a lower tax bracket that will reduce your tax savings. Therefore, when you calculate your savings don't forget to consider the value of the standard deduction. Your real saving is the *difference between* the amount that you would have been taxed had you taken only the standard deduction and the amount you will be taxed if you itemize your deductions.

When you consider your tax savings, suddenly you've got more money that you can use to pay for a mortgage or for repairs or remodeling.

Other Tolls: How Interest Rates Affect Your Mortgage

The size of your mortgage depends not only on your ability to repay the principal, but also on interest rates. The higher the interest rate, the smaller the mortgage you can afford; the lower the interest rate, the larger the mortgage. Because a substantial portion of the price of the home will be covered by the mortgage, interest rates indirectly determine how much you can afford to pay for your new home.

Tollbooth 4.5 shows the amazing variance in the size of a mortgage you can afford depending on the interest rate. The higher the interest rate, the lower the maximum mortgage you will qualify for. This rule of thumb is the reason that it is important to purchase when interest rates are low, if at all possible.

Hazard!

Remember that as time goes by, the amount of your mortgage payment that pays the interest will decrease, and the amount that goes to principal will increase (in a standard amortized mortgage). This shift will affect your tax savings for subsequent years, but you are accumulating equity faster.

Tollbooth 4.5

How Big a Mortgage Your Monthly Payment Will Buy

Mortgage payment of $1,322 for a 30-year fixed mortgage

Rate	Mortgage Amount
5%	$246,000
6%	220,000
7%	200,000
8%	182,000
9%	164,000
10%	151,000

Mortgage payment of $1,322 for a 15 year fixed mortgage

Rate	Mortgage Amount
5%	$167,000
6%	157,000
7%	147,000
8%	138,000
9%	130,000
10%	123,000

Paying the First Toll: How Big a Down Payment Can You Afford?

The size of the mortgage you get and, correspondingly, the amount you can pay for your home depend heavily on the size of your down payment. The larger your down payment, the larger the loan you're likely to qualify for.

Unfortunately, this dynamic is a big trouble spot for most first-time borrowers. After all, your entire down payment must come from savings. You don't have another house that you can sell, so you have no equity to roll over. So how do you come up with a sufficient down payment?

It's probably not a good idea to delay your purchase until you have saved up for a large down payment. In most markets, the longer you wait, the more expensive the houses become. Also, if interest rates are rising, you want to get into the market as soon as possible.

Unfortunately, lenders do not allow you to make the down payment from borrowed money. However, if you borrowed the money a long time ago, say six months or more, the lender usually won't consider it to have been borrowed specifically to make a home purchase, and you might get away with using the borrowed money as your down payment. But extra loan payments will affect your borrowing ability.

As mentioned, parents, grandparents, or other relatives frequently give or loan money to first-time homebuyers to help with the down payment. (Generally, gifts of up to $10,000 annually are nontaxable.) In the past, lenders frowned on these gifts and loans. They do so far less today, although they may still want to get the names of the donors on the mortgage, and they may require them to qualify for it as well.

Finally, it's important to understand that you will need cash for more than the down payment; you will also have to pay closing costs, inspection costs, and other expenses. You may also want to buy some new furniture for your house, and it's best to keep a reserve in case of emergencies. Therefore, you should hold on to as much cash as possible. Of course, the larger your down payment, the smaller your mortgage and your monthly payments, but keep in mind that putting down an extra percent or two won't make much difference in your monthly payments.

Generally speaking, you won't need the full down payment until the deal closes, which usually occurs at the time you move in. It could be a couple of months or more between the time your offer is accepted by the seller and the time the deal closes. However, you'll need to show the lender that you have the money to put down by referring to a savings or similar account. And you'll need to have the escrow deposit available as soon as the seller accepts your offer.

Few people are in the lucky position of being able to put down more money than the lender requires. Most of us strain to get the minimum down payment. If you are fortunate enough to have the option of putting more money down, should you do it? A lot depends on what your goals are. Putting more money down will reduce the amount of your mortgage and, in turn, your monthly payments. But unless you add a huge sum above the minimum amount of the down payment, your monthly payments won't be reduced by much, and you won't have that cash available if you need it for other purposes. (You may, however, be able to obtain a home equity loan (a second mortgage) if you need cash in the future.) You might also qualify for a PMI mortgage, which requires a lower down payment (see page 102 for details).

Which Way to Turn? Types of Mortgages

There is an alphabet soup of mortgages out there. This section briefly describes the two most frequently used mortgages along with their major variations. For more details on these and other types of mortgages not discussed here, see the Resources section in Appendix B.

1. Low Down Payment Mortgages

Because finding the cash is usually the hardest part of most real estate purchases, let's consider mortgages that allow you to put up a minimal down payment. All of these mortgages (with one exception, as we'll see) involve having some sort of guarantee of your past payment performance. That's why you can get away with putting less money down.

FHA Mortgages. The Federal Housing Administration (FHA) insures these mortgages that are available from banks, savings and loans (S&Ls), and mortgage brokers. From the first-time buyer's perspective, FHA mortgages are desirable because the standard down payment is only 5 percent. (In some rural areas and within some special programs, that figure can go as low as 3 percent.) This means that if the house you're purchasing costs $100,000, you only have to come up with $5,000 as a down payment! However, FHA mortgages have some restrictions and other negative aspects.

1. The available mortgage amounts differ from community to community, depending on the median price of homes in your area. If your house is worth much more than the cost of median-priced homes, or if you're in a high-priced area, an FHA loan may not be of much use to you.
2. The FHA loan itself is expensive. There is a loan origination fee, a hefty mortgage insurance premium, and usually additional points.
3. The government requires strict credit and income qualification from applicants, and the house must pass a special FHA inspection.

VA (Veterans Administration) Mortgages. The Department of Veterans Affairs in Washington, D.C., guarantees these mortgages (as opposed to FHA loans that are insured). VA mortgages are available only to veterans of the U.S. Armed Forces who served for a specific number of days during certain periods of time. If you are a qualified veteran, a VA mortgage can be an excellent loan for you because no down payment is required, although you may have to pay something down if the house costs more than the maximum mortgage amount allowed. Because most people just starting out are not retired veterans, we'll move on, but if you are a retired vet, see Appendix B for books with additional information on this topic.

Insured Conventional Mortgages. These loans are the standard conventional mortages. They cover 80 percent of either the appraised value of the home or the selling price, whichever is lower. However, lenders can increase the amount borrowed to 90 percent or even 95 percent in some cases, provided that you have sterling credit and a strong income, the property is in a choice area with strong resale potential, and there is private mortgage insurance (PMI) on the loan.

PMI comes from private companies and covers the first 20 percent of the mortgage. In other words, if the buyer defaults on the loan (that means you), and the lender takes back the property and is unable to sell it for the mortgage amount, PMI will cover up to the first 20 percent of the lender's loss. In most cases, this amount is the entire loss incurred by the lender.

There are, however, some negative features of a PMI mortgage. For example, there is a PMI premium that must be paid each month, which usually adds between .5 and .75 of 1 percent to your regular interest rate, thus increasing your monthly payment.

Seller Financing. This type of loan is often a second mortgage (initially; eventually it goes away when you achieve more than 20 percent equity) that you obtain from the seller, in addition to the new mortgage you acquired from an institutional lender. For example, you may get an 80 percent loan from the bank and a 15 percent loan from the seller. You now can get the property for as little as 5 percent down plus closing costs! And you don't have to be qualified for the second mortgage because it's coming from the seller.

The problem with this type of loan is that sellers usually do not want to give mortgages because of the risk involved. (You might not repay them.). The sellers may also need the cash to buy another property. Thus, while you may find a seller who will "carry back" some "paper" (as these loans are referred to in the trade), it is not likely to happen. In addition, many institutional lenders today set a maximum *combined* loan amount. This means that you may get 80 percent from the lender, but the lender will allow you to borrow only another 10 percent from the seller.

Conforming Loans. Conforming loans adhere to the underwriting standards of Fannie Mae and Freddie Mac, the *secondary lenders* that lend money to the institution that lends to you. Both Fannie Mae and Freddie Mac have a wide variety of low down payment mortgages. Indeed, Fannie Mae has experimented with no down payment mortgages! Ask a mortgage broker for information on their various programs. You may also want to check out their Web sites, which are loaded with information on their various programs: http://www.fanniemae.com and http://www.freddiemac.com.

2. Low Monthly Payment Mortgages

So far, we have examined mortgage types that help a first-time buyer purchase a home with a lower down payment. Now let's consider mortgages that are specifically designed to give you lower monthly payments. (Note that some low monthly payment mortgages can be combined with low down payment mortgages to create a mortgage that offers both. For example, you can combine an adjustable-rate mortgage with a PMI mortgage.)

Adjustable-Rate Mortgage (ARM). An adjustable-rate mortgage can cut your mortgage payment by a third or more, at least in the early days of the mortgage. For example, if your payment is going to be $900 a month with a fixed-rate mortgage, an adjustable-rate mortgage can initially cut that down to $600 a month or even less.

This adjustability has two important ramifications, especially for first-time buyers. First, with a lower monthly payment, you may be able to get into a house and a neighborhood that you would not otherwise qualify for. Second, because you're making a lower monthly payment, it will be easier for you to maintain a higher quality lifestyle. On the other hand, ARMs have some significant drawbacks:

1. The low monthly payments last a relatively short time (months or, at the outside, a few years). After that, the monthly payment can rise (if interest rates rise) quickly to a point at which it's actually higher than if you had opted for a fixed-rate mortgage. Therefore, an ARM is particularly useful if you're planning on living in the home for only a short period of time—let's say, three years or less. The ARM is also useful during periods of temporarily high interest rates because it allows you to get into a property at a lower than market rate when market rates are high. Then, when rates have fallen several years later, you can refinance to a fixed rate mortgage.

2. There is a very low teaser rate, which may be less than half of the market rate, that is designed to get you interested in and hooked on the

mortgage. But the teaser rate doesn't last long; typically it's seldom longer than one year, and sometimes it's as short as one month. After that, the interest rate begins to "adjust" (hence the name *adjustable*-rate mortgage) to market conditions: It rises and continues to rise at set adjustment periods, usually once, at most twice a year, until it's at (or usually slightly above) market rate. As a result, your mortgage, which may have started out at 4 percent, can quickly double its interest rate. At the end of the first year, you may be paying twice as much!

3. How high the interest rate goes is determined in part by the index used and the margin. Make sure that the lender shows you a 20-year history of each index. Depending on your needs, you may want to select one that has been stable or one that has been volatile. Let's say the index is at 6 percent and the lender arbitrarily tacks on a margin of 3 percent. Therefore, your adjusted interest rate will be 9 percent. Obviously, if the index goes down, so, too, will your interest rate. But if the index goes up, your interest rate will also increase.

   At the beginning of your mortgage when you have the teaser rate, your true interest rate will be much higher. For example, your teaser rate may be 4 percent, but your true interest rate may be 9 percent. That means that at the time of each adjustment period, your rate will rise the full step until it reaches 9 percent. Then, for some ARMs, the rate will continue to rise for a period of time until you make up the interest lost by the lender when your rate was below the market rate! In short, you don't gain anything in the long run, and you may lose if rates go up. But if you sell before the rates rise, you could save a great deal of money.

4. Many ARMs offer caps on the interest rate, which means that the interest rate cannot rise beyond a certain maximum. The cap is typically 4–6 percent above the current market interest rate, so there's relatively little chance the mortgage will get that high, unless there's runaway inflation in the country. The cap is a "feel good" sort of thing, but it's rarely going to be helpful.

   Other mortgages offer caps on the monthly payment. They guarantee that the monthly payment will not rise beyond a certain point. Again, this feature is designed to make you feel good about taking the mortgage. The problem is that if the interest rate rises to the point at which your monthly payment is higher than the cap, the difference that you're not paying is usually added on to your principal. Because the difference is added to the mortgage amount, you pay interest on that interest in the future! This is called negative amortization and should be avoided by first-time buyers. It's a perfect definition of an "ugly" mortgage.

ARMs are complex mortgages. For more information on ARMs, see Appendix B.

Graduated Payment Mortgage (GPM). This type of mortgage is designed specifically for first-time homebuyers. It has a low initial interest rate that increases by incremental steps at designated periods of time (usually every year or so). Each step raises the interest rate and monthly payments by predetermined amounts. Eventually, perhaps seven years down the road, the interest rate is higher than the market rate was when you made your purchase.

The idea behind the GPM is that as you get older and as your income grows, so, too, will the mortgage payment. You will have low payments when you first start out, and then later, as you're more able to pay, you'll pay more. Unlike an ARM, in which the mortgage adjusts according to an index and the amount of future payments is unknown, the GPM is a fixed interest rate mortgage with a rate that changes at predetermined times and in predetermined amounts.

If you see yourself on a career course that will provide you with increasing income, a GPM could be a good mortgage for you. The problem, of course, is that the payment schedule is inflexible, and if your career nosedives, you might not be able to make the higher monthly payments, causing you to lose your house.

On the good side, however, you never have to worry about negative amortization with a GPM. And you won't get any shocks. You'll know well in advance what every monthly payment will be. GPMs are often combined with FHA mortgages. Ask your lender for more information about them in your area.

Short-Term Mortgages. This type of mortgage is often recommended to first-time buyers because it combines the best features of the adjustable-rate mortgage and the fixed-rate mortgage. Short-term mortgages have two different time periods: an initial loan period and a secondary loan period. Generally during the initial time period, there is a lower than market rate, fixed-rate mortgage. During the secondary time period, there is a rather ugly adjustable-rate mortgage.

For example, the current market rate may be 8 percent. Let's say you get a three-year mortgage. During the first three years of your mortgage, your payments may be based on a 7 percent interest rate amortized (paid in equal payments) over 30 years, just as if you had a true 30-year, fixed-rate mortgage. You save 1 percent for the three years. At the end of the third year, however, the mortgage either comes due as a balloon or converts to an adjustable-rate mortgage with a high margin and a volatile index. At this point you usually end up paying more than market rate interest. That's when you refinance or sell.

The advantage is that you will know in advance what your monthly payment will be for a fixed period of time. If you're like most people, you would probably plan to sell before that time period ends, and hence you would get the benefits without incurring the drawback of the high adjustable interest rate.

Interest-Only Loans. This type of loan is a fixed-rate mortgage, so instead of paying interest plus principal each month, you pay only interest. However, because of amortization (payback) of loans, this amounts to only a small monthly savings, perhaps in the neighborhood of less than 5 percent of the monthly payment. (Most of the interest is paid at the beginning of a mortgage, most of the principal paid at the end.) If you're not planning to keep the property long and want a slightly lower fixed-rate mortgage, this is an option you might consider.

Balloon-Payment Mortgage. A balloon-payment mortgage will sometimes earn a first-time buyer a lower interest rate and, therefore, a lower monthly payment. But beware: You could end up losing your house if you don't take timely action. A balloon mortgage is any type of mortgage that is not fully amortized, which means it is not paid off in equal payments. Homeowners usually carry such a loan for a fairly short time (five years or so), during which they make payments only on the interest. At the end of a specified period of time, the mortgage is all due in one huge (balloon) payment—that is, you must come up with the cash or refinance.

▶ Which Road to Take: Condo, Co-Op, Townhome, or House?

Now you know something about the various types of mortgages. If you don't think you can afford to buy a house, or if you think you don't need all that room, then you might consider buying a condominium, a co-operative, or a townhome (also called a townhouse). These options are all excellent choices for homebuyers just starting out. All three types of housing can be sound investments, comfortable, affordable, and full of amenities. They're also great stepping stones to larger properties that you should be able to afford later on down the road. Before we go any further, let's settle on a few basic definitions, courtesy of *Barron's Real Estate Handbook*:

▶ a condominium or condo is a system of ownership of individual units in a multiunit structure combined with joint ownership of commonly used property, such as sidewalks, hallways, and stairs.

▶ a cooperative or co-op is housing in which each tenant is a shareholder in the corporation that owns a building.

▶ a *townhome* is a dwelling, usually with two or more floors, attached to other similar units by common walls called "party walls."

What are the differences? Condos and co-ops are quite different:

▶ When purchasing a condo, you're truly buying real estate. It's solid property that you can touch, such as walls, floors, and ceilings, but you do not purchase the land.

▶ When you buy a co-op, you're not buying land or property; you're buying shares in a company as if you were buying shares of GE, Ford, Microsoft, or of a mutual fund. You may live on the property, but you don't really own the specific roof over your head, the dirt beneath your floor, or the space around you. Taxes are paid by the property owner (the corporation), although this expense is passed on as part of your monthly maintenance. Of course, this amount is tax deductible. As a corporation, a co-op has a board of directors who have the power to approve or reject potential investors according to each individual's or family's income level or personal character. The board, however, cannot make decisions that violate the nation's civil rights laws.

▶ Townhomes and condos have much in common; in fact, in many cases townhomes are designated by law as condominiums. Owners of townhomes usually, though not always, own the land on which their property rests.

Many real estate experts predict that the comparatively low price of condos will continue to attract buyers for some time. Clearly, ease of entry into the market and appreciation of that investment are primary factors in the rising popularity of condos.

On the Road of Life, Money Is Not the Only Factor

Finally, in addition to all the financial issues to consider when deciding whether to rent or buy, there are also lifestyle issues that may influence your decision. At the beginning of this chapter, we mentioned that if you're planning to relocate in a few years (or if you even think you might), you probably should rent until you settle in one place long enough to make it worthwhile to buy. But relocation is not the only issue.

Buying a single-family home is also work. When you buy a house, you buy a lawn and lawns have to be mowed, landscaped, raked in the fall, and re-seeded in the spring. Lawns are the things your neighbors are always working on while you're slothfully sitting inside watching a baseball game. The lawn is the thing you have to stay home to work on while your neighbors are heading out to the golf course.

Picture this. It's a hot summer Saturday afternoon. You're sitting in the shade in the backyard of your single-family dwelling while enjoying a cold glass of lemonade, iced tea, or your favorite adult beverage. Life is good. Then you notice that the grass has grown a little too high. The flowerbed needs weeding and leaves are choking your rain gutters. Well, there goes the pleasant afternoon. It's time to break out the lawn mower, the garden hoe, the ladder, and other tools. You'll probably be breaking out a lot of sweat, too.

The same thing can happen on a cold winter Saturday afternoon. You're sitting all toasty warm in front of a roaring television set sipping hot cocoa, hot tea, or your favorite adult beverage. Life is good. Then you notice that the snow has covered your walkway. Ice has accumulated on your steps, and an icy breeze is slipping under the front door. It's time to break out the snow shovel, the rock salt, and the weather stripping and say good-bye to that ball game you wanted to watch.

If you don't want to do this much work, then you should consider buying a condo, co-op, or townhome because the association you buy into will handle all those chores. The association is a great resource when your property needs maintenance or repair. You may need a plumbing fixture replaced, a room painted, a crack in the ceiling or a broken window repaired, or any number of problems handled. Instead of getting your hands dirty, scraping your knuckles, and bumping your head and cursing, all you have to do as a member of the association is make a phone call and wait for the plumber, electrician, carpenter, landscaper, or other professional to show up and take care of the problem.

In addition, the professionals will probably have some history with your building: They'll probably know the customs and traditions of the property and the people living there. Because a condo, co-op, or townhome association represents such a large amount of work (and profit) for a home professional, it commands far greater loyalty and response than is usually available to any individual, which is a huge plus when a city gets bogged down in an ice storm and everyone in town is screaming for service. Who's going to get the fastest response: the lone homeowner in the suburbs or the 500-member condo association down the street? Having this kind of convenience sure beats flipping through the Yellow Pages and then trying to cajole tradespeople to put you at the top of their lists.

The real draw for condos, co-ops, and townhomes for many people is the simple fact that someone else has the responsibility for doing the chores. The appearance of your property will be maintained, and needed repairs will be made but not by you.

In addition to the work involved in buying property, you are also buying responsibility. You buy property taxes and building codes, sewer systems or septic tanks, and flooded basements and leaky roofs. When you buy a home, you buy adulthood. Nothing says you're grown up like owning a home of your own. As a MasterCard commercial might say, "A ceiling leak from a broken upstairs water pipe: $1,800. A hot water heater busted in the morning: $1,000. A toilet overflows: $80. Being able to call the landlord: priceless."

On the other hand, owning your own home is just about the coolest thing on the planet. Having a patch of ground and being able to say, "This is mine," is one of the greatest things you are ever going to say in this world. Home ownership means you have control over the four corners of a piece of property.

As long as you're a renter, no matter how long you live there, you are living in someone else's building and according to someone else's rules. You are living on someone else's property. No matter what the lease says, you're a guest there, and there are going to be limits, even self-imposed limits that are born of civil behavior that you are going to have to adhere to.

When you own your own home, if you want to dig a three-foot hole in your front yard, you can do it. If you want to poke a hole through an interior wall and put in a window between two rooms, you can do it. If you want to put pink flamingos all over your yard; well, it might not be a good idea, but you can do it.

In short, there's a real pleasure to being master of your castle. You can put a nail in the wall to hang a picture without worrying that you might not get all of your security deposit back. If you want a pet, you don't have to be concerned about what the neighbor next door will say. In short, there's a kind of freedom that comes with home ownership that tenants never get to experience. But you have to decide how much freedom you want—and how much responsibility, including financial responsibility.

Learn the Language

Key Terms to Know When Buying a Home

Adjustable-rate mortgage (ARM) A mortgage tied to an index that increases or decreases based on changes in the economy.

Amortization The process of retiring a debt by making predetermined periodic payments on both the principal and the interest.

Balloon payment A large payment on a principal sum that comes due at a predetermined time (may also contain payment of accrued interest).

Convertible ARM An adjustable-rate mortgage that contains a clause allowing the interest rate to become fixed for a certain period during the life of the loan; for example, between months 13 and 60 of the loan term.

Credit scoring The practice of assigning a numerical value to various financial factors in the borrower's credit to determine the risk of lending to that borrower.

Debt ratios The comparison of buyers' housing costs to their gross or net effective income (based on the loan program), and the comparison of buyers' total long-term debt to their gross or net effective income (based on the loan program used). The first ratio is termed *housing ratio;* the second ratio is *total debt ratio.* (*See* particular programs for applicable ratios.)

Equity The difference between the amount that the buyer owes on a property and the amount that property can be sold for.

Escrow An impartial holding of documents pertinent to the sale and transfer of real estate; also the term used to describe the long-term holding of documents, as occurs in seller financing (also called a long-term escrow or escrow collection).

Fannie Mae Foundation A nonprofit foundation affiliated with the FNMA, designed to educate consumers on home affordability and homebuying options.

FHLMC Federal Home Loan Mortgage Corporation, also known as Freddie Mac, a part of the secondary market that is usually used to purchase loans from S&L (Savings and Loan) lenders within the Federal Home Loan Bank Board.

FHA Federal Housing Administration, part of the federal government's Department of Housing and Urban Development. This agency exists to underwrite insured loans made by lenders to provide economical housing for moderate-income persons.

FNMA Federal National Mortgage Association, also known as Fannie Mae, a privately owned part of the secondary mortgage market used to recycle mortgages made in the primary market. FNMA purchases conventional, FHA, and VA loans.

FRM Fixed-rate mortgage, a conventional loan with a single interest rate for the life of the loan.

FICO The Fair, Isaac & Company credit scoring system used by many lenders to determine a borrower's ability to repay a mortgage. FICO uses a scoring range of 300 to 850: the lower the score, the higher the lending risk.

GNMA Government National Mortgage Association, also known as Ginnie Mae, a governmental part of the secondary market that deals primarily in recycling VA and FHA mortgages, particularly those that are highly leveraged (a low or no down payment).

PITI Acronym used by mortgage lenders that includes principal, interest, taxes (on property), and insurance.

Points A point is equal to 1 percent of the mortgage amount financed. Points are used to increase the lender's yield on the loan to bridge the gap between what the lender could get with conventional monies and the lower rates of the VA and the FHA mortgages.

Seller financing The seller allows the borrower to finance the property, using a portion of the seller's equity in the property.

Travel in Style

Buying a Car

Along with purchasing a home and funding college tuition, buying a car numbers among the largest single investment you may ever make. Long gone are the days when you could spend $5,000 for an economy car that would last for years. Today cars come in a multitude of styles and price ranges that offer an incredible array of options.

The process of buying a car is composed of two separate but related steps. First, you must determine your transportation needs and the type of car that will best meet them. Second, you need to decide how you will pay for the car. A car purchase entails weighing the pros and cons of dealer or bank financing, leasing, and paying cash. This chapter will guide you in both choosing your car and paying for it.

▶ Before Hitting the Road: Determine What Type of Car You Need

Before you visit a dealer's showroom or pick up your first car review magazine, carefully evaluate your transportation needs. By writing down the features you want in a car and how much you can spend, you can avoid making a hasty or costly decision that you will regret later. Many buyers have had their emotions overtake their common sense, leaving them with beautiful, option-filled cars that boost their self-esteem but take large bites out of their wallets.

Here are 15 questions you should consider when deciding what kind of car to buy:

1. How long do you plan to keep the car?
2. Will you use it mostly for short local trips or for long drives?
3. How important is good gas mileage? (In general, the more luxurious the car, the poorer its gas mileage.)
4. If you have children: What will your family's transportation needs be in the short and long term?
5. If you do not have children: Do you anticipate having children during the years that you will own the car? What will be your family's transportation needs then?
6. How many passengers will normally use the car? What is the maximum number of people the car will need to carry?
7. What types of storage will you need? Will you often carry groceries from the supermarket, or will you frequently lug heavy suitcases as well? Do you need a storage rack on top of the car as well as ample trunk space?
8. Will you tow trailers behind the car? If so, how big will they be? (If you rent large trailers regularly, you will need a car with more horsepower. Otherwise, rent the car, too.)
9. What facilities are available at home, at work, or at a train or bus station for parking the car?
10. How safe are the neighborhoods where you will park the car? (Answering this question will help you determine how expensive a car to acquire, the types of anti-theft devices it will require, and how essential a garage will be.)
11. How important is car safety? Will you pay a premium for a very safe car? (Though you may pay a bigger one for an unsafe car.)
12. How important is comfort? (Today's automakers offer many luxurious features that are nice to have but cost thousands of dollars.)
13. How much attention are you willing to give toward the car's maintenance? (You may be a car buff who relishes the thought of tuning and waxing your beauty every Saturday. Or your definition of maintenance might be telling a gas station attendant to check the oil.)

14. What are the weather and road conditions where you will drive the car? For example, do you live in an area so hot during the summer that air-conditioning is a must? Will you drive the vehicle off paved roads or in a hilly area? If so, four-wheel drive will be necessary.

15. Which options are vital and which are expendable? Many options are available, but you'll pay for each one, from an adjustable steering column and an air bag for the passenger seat to upholstery options and windshield heating systems. So think about what you really need.

Hazard!
Don't Forget to Consider the Cost of Owning a Car

In addition to all the other practical and lifestyle considerations that can affect the cost of your car, don't forget to carefully consider how much you want to (or can afford to) spend annually for car insurance, annual inspections, gasoline, and routine maintenance costs as well as major repairs that will probably be required during the lifetime of your car.

Taking a Test Drive: The Car Shopping Process

Now that you've considered your lifestyle issues, determined which options are most important to you, and decided how much you want to spend each year on gasoline, it's time to set a target price for the car you want to buy. Because you won't know exactly which car is right for you until you've shopped around, set a wide range at first, perhaps in increments of $5,000. You should have an idea of whether you can afford a car for $10,000–$15,000, $15,000–$20,000, or above $20,000.

Once you've chosen a price range, your options will narrow quickly. Consult magazines like *Motor Trend* and *Car and Driver* to learn more about the models that interest you. For a complete write-up of all cars, consult the April auto issue of *Consumer Reports* or its *New Car Buying Guide* (see the Appendix for details). The latter is a definitive and unbiased guide, updated every year, based on the results of the extensive testing of all new cars as reported in *Consumer Reports* magazine. For data on the injury records and collision losses of car manufacturers' various models, contact the Highway Loss Data Institute. Edmunds.com is another great resource. You can find out lots about a car, including what the dealer paid, cash rebates, or incentives available. (For details, see Appendix B.)

As soon as you've selected a few cars that meet your criteria, visit a dealership for a test drive or drop by a local auto show to better compare the vehicles. If you visit a dealer, tell the salesperson that you are considering several models and only want to test drive. Don't buy anything yet! To make sure you're getting the best car and deal for your money, here are a few other things you should ask when you're shopping. The anwers may ultimately affect the amount you pay for your car and its maintainenance.

What does the warranty cover? Automakers now compete aggressively to offer the longest and most complete warranties, and you should benefit from this competition. Auto warranties often last for either three years or 36,000 miles, or five years or 50,000 miles (in both cases, whichever comes first).

Is an extended warranty available? In addition to offering basic warranties, most automakers offer extended warranties or service contracts. The extended warranty goes into effect when the basic warranty lapses. However, most extended service contracts are not good deals. They can be quite expensive, and they contain so many exclusions that you often find they do not cover what has broken. Many extended warranties also require a deductible each time you bring in your car for repair. In addition, the extended service contract often duplicates the basic warranty coverage, and many of the extended warranty's other provisions, such as towing service and car rental during repairs, are covered by your basic auto insurance policy or membership in an auto club.

Who supports the service contract? If you still want a service contract, make sure that you know who backs it: the auto manufacturer, the dealer, or an independent company called an *administrator* that uses claims adjusters to authorize the payment of claims to the dealer. If the dealer or an administrator backs the warranty, find out who will fulfill your extended service if one or both of them go out of business. In some cases, the contract is also backed by an insurance company that would pick up any expenses if your primary service agent is unable to do so. Check to see whether the service contract is transferable if you sell the car. Sometimes the service company charges a fee to transfer the contract. If you consider buying a service contract, wait several months after you purchase the car to determine whether the vehicle is likely to need many repairs.

The High Road: Closing the Deal on a New Car

After you've narrowed your search to one or two models, it's time to concentrate on getting the best price. The easiest way to accomplish this goal is to arm yourself with knowledge of the dealer's cost. You should bargain from the dealer's cost upward, not the sticker price downward. Typically the dealer will settle for a profit margin from 3–7 percent greater than the dealer's cost if the car is not in high demand. That difference might amount to $200 to $500 more than the dealer paid. The suggested retail price might build in a profit margin as high as 12 percent.

If several dealers operate in your neighborhood, bargain with all of them, and play one off against another. Dealers often brag that they offer the lowest prices in town, so make them prove it. On the other hand, if the car you want is a hot seller, you have less bargaining power and may have to pay close to the suggested retail price. Other ways to look for a good deal on a car include checking prices in the classified ads in newspapers. You may also wish to visit used car dealers and car rental agencies that might offer the same model, slightly used or a year old, for thousands of dollars less than the price of a new car.

Although you might not endear yourself to the salesperson by knowing the dealership's costs, most dealers have come to expect this knowledge from cost-conscious consumers. Four services can tell you a dealer's cost for every model and all options:

▶ Edmunds.com
▶ CarBargains
▶ Consumer Reports Auto Price Service
▶ *Money* Magazine's Auto Cost Comparison

(Details on these services are provided in the "Resources" section in Appendix B.) The services also provide data on projected repair histories, annual expenses, and manufacturers' incentives or rebate programs that are currently in effect. Salespeople at local dealerships may contest the numbers on the printouts from these services, but the figures are updated continuously and are accurate.

Hazard!

Make Sure You Understand All Levels of Pricing a Car before You Negotiate

Determining the price you should bargain from can often be confusing. Dealers refer to the following four prices:

The *invoice price* is the price the automaker charges the dealer. It always includes *freight,* or what are commonly called destination and delivery charges. The dealer's actual cost may be less than the invoice price because of rebates, incentives, and other discounts.

- ► The *base price* is the cost of the car with standard equipment and a basic warranty but no options.
- ► The *Monroney sticker price* is the price listed on the sticker attached to the car window. It includes the base price, the cost of installed options, destination charges, and fuel economy information.
- ► The *dealer sticker price* equals the Monroney sticker price plus the suggested retail price of any options installed by the dealer.

If you hate to haggle, you might use an auto broker or a buyer's service to obtain a good price. Brokers usually buy a high volume of cars through a dealer's fleet sales department, and can therefore obtain a better deal than you could get on your own. Brokers usually take possession of the car first and then resell it to you. However, dealing with brokers has a few drawbacks. For example, brokers usually do not accept trade-ins, tend to work with a limited number of dealers, and cannot find all models of all car makes. You can locate local brokers through your local Yellow Pages, or you may find one through the largest national organization of auto brokers, Nationwide Auto Brokers (29623 Northwestern Hwy., Southfield, MI 48034; 1-248-354-3400 (http://www.nationwide-auto.com).

In contrast to brokers, buyer's services can usually work with all makes and models in all 50 states. These services do not take possession of the vehicle. After the buyer's service has found a factory-authorized dealer that will give you the lowest price, you buy directly from the dealer. Buyer's services can also handle trade-ins. Two of the biggest buyer's services are offered by the American Automobile Association and AutoAdvisor, Inc. (See the "Resources" section in Appendix B for more information.)

When negotiating to buy a new car, limit the conversation to the car's price until you agree on a deal. Do not discuss trade-in allowances for your existing car, rebates, or financing options until the price is firm. Many dealers will extract a higher price from you by giving you less than your old car is worth or by adjusting financing terms. To get an idea of your trade-in's value, consult the *N.A.D.A. Official Used Car Guide,* Retail Edition (discussed in more detail in Appendix B) and *Edmund's Used Car Prices,* available on most newsstands, or Edmunds.com.

Although most dealers expect to haggle over price, GM's Saturn division created the trend of buying from a *fixed-price dealer.* These dealers are not allowed to sell the car for less than the suggested retail price, which is supposedly marked down to prevent the need for bargaining. However, you still have to negotiate the value of your trade-in. When you have agreed on a price, a trade-in allowance, and financing terms, don't drop your guard. Read the fine print in your sales agreement and make sure you understand everything in it. (You might want to bring along a magnifying glass!) If you have a question, ask. Don't rely on oral promises, and don't sign a contract containing blank spaces. Make sure that you can get your deposit back if the car delivered to you does not meet your standards. It's best to have the manager of the dealership as well as the salesperson sign the sales agreement to ensure that the contract is legally binding.

Once you've signed the contract, you have plenty of paperwork to complete before you can drive your new car out of the dealer's lot. The details on these forms are beyond the scope of this book, but here's what you or the dealer must obtain:

▶ title forms
▶ registration certificate
▶ license plates
▶ proof of insurance
▶ proof of sales tax payment
▶ inspection sticker

The Low Road: Buying a Used Car

Most of the advice about buying a new car also pertains to buying a used car. Here are a few extra tips. First, choose from among the following five sources of used cars that best suits your needs:

1. *New car dealers usually sell the cars they have purchased as trade-ins.* The cars have often been repaired in the firm's service department before being offered for sale, and they may provide a limited warranty.
2. *Used car dealers usually sell cars with more mileage and wear and tear than the trade-ins on new car dealers' lots.* Used car dealers may offer limited warranties.
3. *Car rental agencies offer vehicles that have been rented for several months, (perhaps as long as six months) and that have driven 8,000–15,000 miles.* Because the cars have been used by many drivers, they probably are not as well cared for as cars driven by one person. However, the car's history is reflected in the price, which means that you can get a good deal.
4. *Banks sell repossessed cars to pay off defaulted loans.* The vehicles can often be purchased at auctions or directly through the banks. The quality of your deal depends totally on how well the previous owner cared for the car.
5. *Individuals sell their cars through newspaper ads.* Have the car checked out thoroughly by a mechanic before you buy it because you may not receive any warranties or other protections once you purchase the vehicle. When you've located a car that interests you, examine the following features carefully. Although they are not financial factors, you'll pay in the long run if you don't check them out well before you buy:

   ▶ battery (Check the date purchased and conduct a power test.)
   ▶ body (Check for damage, repairs, rust, and welding.)
   ▶ doors and window glass (operation, rattle)
   ▶ fluids, such as oil and radiator and transmission fluid (clear, full, leakage)
   ▶ heater and air conditioner (leakage, noises, operation)
   ▶ interior upholstery (clean, holes)
   ▶ lights (headlight alignment, operation)
   ▶ radio (operation)
   ▶ shock absorbers or struts (damage, leakage)
   ▶ tailpipe (connectors, holes, rust)
   ▶ tires (sidewall, tread, wear)

Finally, test drive the car extensively to check the steering, brakes, and other major systems. While you drive, pay attention to unusual vibrations, noises, or odors, which could be tip-offs to larger problems.

Once you've found a car that passes all these tests, bargain with the seller as you would with the salesperson at a new car dealership. Use as a guide the prices listed in the National Automobile Dealers Association's *N.A.D.A. Official Used Car Guide.* (See Appendix B for details.) The book provides a low, a high, and an average retail price for most used cars.

Choose Your Tollbooth: Financing vs. Leasing a Car

The most inexpensive way to buy your new car is to pay cash because you then have no financing costs. However, most people can't come up with $10,000 to $30,000 or more in cash at one time. That leaves two main options: financing and leasing. Tollbooth 5.1 offers a quick comparative overview, and the following sections offer more details.

The Ins and Outs of Car Loans

Obtaining a car loan was much more attractive in the days when consumer interest was fully tax deductible. However, today many low-interest options are available to qualified buyers.

The monthly loan payment includes loan fees, the payment that the lender paid to obtain your credit report, and charges for *credit life insurance.* This type of insurance will pay off the auto loan for you if you die with a balance due. Most financial advisors recommend against taking credit life coverage because it is very expensive and your regular life insurance should pay your bills if you die prematurely.

When shopping for the best loan, look at the *annual percentage rate* (APR); that is, the interest rate you pay each year on the unpaid loan balance. To some extent, the interest rate, or the APR that you get on your car loan, will depend on your credit history. The more creditworthy you are, the lower your rate will be.

In addition to looking at the interest rate, determine the amount of the down payment each lender requires. If your trade-in does not cover the down payment, most lenders ask for between 10 percent and 20 percent of the value of the car you're buying, depending on your creditworthiness. The less you invest up front, the higher your financing costs and monthly payments will be over time. All lenders require that the total loan be covered by collateral: namely, your car. If you miss a few payments, you lose your car to repossession.

Several sources for car loans exist. They are described in the following sections.

Tollbooth 5.1

Cost Comparison for Leasing vs. Buying and Financing a Car

Feature	Leasing	Buying and Financing
Down payment	None or small	Usually required; the more that's paid up front, the smaller the monthly payment
Monthly payments	Continuous, usually less than for buying	End when the loan is paid off
Vehicle modification	Not allowed	You can do what you want, when you want
Mileage limits	Usually 12,000 to 15,000 miles/year	Unlimited
Wear and tear	If in excess of contract limits, penalties due at end of lease	No limits
Early termination	Fees and penalties apply	There usually are no prepayment penalties
End of term	Lease again, or purchase the currently leased vehicle; payments continue	Payments stop
Ownership	None	Ownership equity builds with each payment. Vehicle is owned at the end of the financing period.

Dealers. Car dealers offer financing, often through the so-called captive finance arm of the automaker. Expect a GM dealer to direct you to the General Motors Acceptance Corporation (GMAC), a Ford dealer to suggest Ford Credit, and so on. Usually, the interest rates charged by captive finance companies are higher than those available at local banks or credit unions. However, for many buyers, this type of financing may be the only available credit source depending on their level of credit risk. Dealers push financing with captive finance companies because they receive money for every car loan

Hazard!

Financing from Automakers Comes with Strings Attached

In the most extreme cases, captive finance companies (such as Ford Credit, available when you buy a Ford) tout 0 percent financing. It's hard to beat 0 percent interest, except that such deals often come with many strings attached, and you must pay a higher price for the car than if you financed it through another source or paid cash.

Many low-interest loans apply only to cars on the dealer's lot, not to cars ordered with special options from the factory. In many cases, these low-rate loans cover short terms of two or three years, which raises the monthly loan payments significantly. And often they require down payments of 25–30 percent instead of the normal 10 percent. Some dealers require you to surrender the manufacturer's rebate (if there is one) if you obtain a low-interest loan.

they arrange. If car sales are slow, and the manufacturer wants to stimulate buying, it will sweeten financing deals considerably.

Local banks. Your local bank will frequently offer lower interest rates on car loans than dealers. For a detailed listing of low loan rates, consult *Bank Rate Monitor* (http://www.bankrate.com) Telephone: 1-561-630-2400; P.O. Box 088888, North Palm Beach, FL 33408). This publication tracks car loan rates at most banks in the country on a weekly basis.

Credit Unions. If you belong to a credit union, you might obtain an even better loan. Unlike banks, credit unions are designed to serve their members rather than shareholders. As a result, they often charge lower interest rates and offer more lenient terms. In many cases, however, credit unions require larger down payments than banks or finance companies.

The Leasing Alternative

Before you obtain an auto loan, investigate leasing a car. Leasing contracts can be tricky, but you can come out ahead if you lease instead of financing a car, though usually if you keep your cars only a short while, e.g., 3 years. That's why every year more people lease their cars instead of buying them.

Two kinds of leases exist: closed-end and open-end. A *closed-end lease,* often called a *walk-away lease,* allows you to return the car when the agreement expires and walk away without any further responsibility. The leasing company assumes all the risks and headaches of reselling the car. You must, however, return the car in good condition, which includes normal wear and tear. If your lease specified a limit to the number of miles you could drive the car during the agreement, you must make sure that you have not exceeded that limit. If you do exceed it, you must pay a penalty of up to $.15 per mile—which can really add up fast! (When you sign the lease, do not agree to fewer miles than you would normally drive if you owned the car.) Because you are not responsible for the car's worth when the lease terminates, your monthly payments will usually be higher with a closed-end lease than with the open-end variety.

Closed-end leases usually give the leasing company the right to sell the car when the lease expires if you don't want to buy the vehicle. You should obtain a provision in your contract stating that you must approve the sales price. According to most leases, if the company receives less than the residual value (what the car is worth when the lease is up), you must make up the difference. Usually, though, dealers will not force you to make this payment because it alienates you as a customer. When your lease expires, you are a prime candidate to lease another car; therefore, the dealer wants to keep you happy.

An *open-end lease* exposes you to the risk of your car's resale value when the lease expires. When you enter into an open-end lease, you're betting that the car will be worth a certain amount when the lease ends. When you return the car to the leasing company, it is appraised to determine its current market value. If you disagree with the appraisal, you usually have the right to acquire your own independent appraisal from a local car dealer or car appraisal service. Once you and the leasing company agree on the car's value, you compare that amount to the residual value assumed in the lease contract. If the car's value is equal to or greater than the residual value, you owe nothing. Depending on your contract, you may even receive a refund if the appraisal value is considerably more than the residual value.

However, if the appraisal value is less than the residual value, you must make up most or all of the difference in cash, depending on the terms of your lease contract. For example, if your contract assumes the car will have a residual value of $10,000 and the appraisal says it is worth $9,000 when the lease ends, you owe the leasing company $1,000. This settlement is usually referred to as a *balloon payment*. Most open-end leases also give you a purchase option; that is, the right to buy the car at residual value. These are known as *lease-purchase contracts*.

Many companies offer leases. Banks, credit unions, companies that specialize in leasing, and captive finance companies of auto dealers all compete for auto leases. Therefore, shop around for the lease that offers the most favorable terms. Bargain just as hard for good lease terms as you would for the best price on a new or used car. You don't have to accept a leasing company's first offer, just as you don't have to pay a car's sticker price.

The federal Consumer Leasing Act, administered by the Federal Trade Commission, provides certain protections for consumers entering both closed- and open-ended leases. For example, the balloon payment you make in an open-ended lease can never be more than three times your monthly lease payment unless the car has suffered far more damage than could be described as normal wear and tear. This law also requires that you be told the following information:

1. the size of any security deposit due at the beginning of the lease
2. the date each payment is due and the amount your payments will total over the term of the lease
3. the amount you must pay for licenses, car registrations, taxes, and maintenance costs
4. the type of auto insurance required
5. the warranties that will cover the car
6. the person or company that is responsible for maintaining the car, and exactly what is meant by normal wear and tear
7. the consequences of losing your car to theft or an accident. (Some contracts consider a stolen car to be an early termination of the lease and force you to pay fees in excess of the insurance settlement.)
8. the penalties for making late lease payments or defaulting on the contract
9. the possibility of terminating the lease before it is scheduled to expire. (If you bail out early, you will probably have to pay some kind of penalty, which should be specified in your contract.)
10. under what conditions you or the leasing company can cancel the contract

11. the price you will pay for the car if you wish to purchase it when the lease expires
12. the possibility of renewing the lease once it has expired. (Some dealers will offer lower lease payments if you ask for a contract extension clause.)

To decide whether to lease or finance your car, add up the following costs as well as the others listed on the "Leasing Costs Worksheet" in Tollbooth 5.2:

▶ *The security deposit, required up front.* This money can be retained by the leasing company if you fail to make a payment, or if you owe a balloon payment at the termination of the lease. It can also be applied toward

Tollbooth 5.2

Leasing Costs Worksheet

Leasing Costs

Security Deposit	$_____
First Lease Payment	_____
Last Lease Payment	_____
Monthly Lease Payment	_____
Down Payment	_____
Sales Taxes	_____
Registration Fees	_____
Title Fees	_____
License Fees	_____
Insurance Premiums	_____
Dealer-Provided Maintenance Costs	_____
Default Charges	_____
Excess Mileage Charges	_____
Excess Wear-and-Tear Charges	_____
Final Disposition Charges	_____
Balloon Payments	_____
Total leasing costs	_____

the repair of damages to the car or to mileage charges if you exceed your limit. If you owe none of this money when the lease expires, the leasing company should return your deposit.

► *The first and last monthly lease payment, typically required up front.*

► *The down payment, also called the capitalized cost reduction.* The larger the down payment, the less your monthly lease costs. Because one main advantage of leasing is the low up-front, out-of-pocket cost, keep the down payment as low as possible. Some dealers will permit you to use the trade-in value of your old car to make the down payment. However, make sure that they give you a value close to the amount for which you could sell the car in the open market.

► *Fees and maintenance charges, which include sales tax, registration, title and license fees, and insurance premiums.* In some cases leasing dealers will include repair and maintenance costs in your lease if you promise to bring the car into the dealership on a regular basis for a checkup.

► *The costs of concluding the lease, which include default charges, excess mileage and wear-and-tear fees, and balloon payments.* Some dealers will also levy *final disposition charges* for cleaning, tuning, and making final repairs on the car.

Now compare these leasing costs to the annual outlays for financing a new car with a bank or finance company loan (as listed on the Car Loan Worksheet in Tollbooth 5.3).

Choosing between leasing and financing a car is not purely a financial decision. First, determine how long you plan to own the car. If you like to replace your car every three or four years, leasing might make more sense than buying. As you pay off your loan, you will accumulate equity in your car, though that may not be desirable if you plan to trade it in within two to three years. On the other hand, if you plan to hold onto your car for 7 to 10 years or so, buying makes more sense than leasing.

If you expect your transportation needs to change over the next few years, leasing might be the better option. For example, if you plan to have children or add to your family, you might need a larger car in three or four years. Consider how much you will drive the car. If you drive more than 15,000 miles a year, leasing can be very expensive, and buying probably makes more sense. On the other hand, if you use your car only for short runs to the supermarket or the train station, leasing might be preferable. In addition, if you plan to use your car partly for business, you can deduct a portion of your lease

Tollbooth 5.3

Car Loan Worksheet

Car Loan Costs

Down Payment	$_____
Monthly Interest Costs	_____
Sales Taxes	_____
License Fees	_____
Registration Fees	_____
Insurance Premiums	_____
Estimated Maintenance Charges	_____
Trade-in Allowances	_____
Total car loan costs	_____

payments as a business expense, which you cannot do if you purchase the car, although you can deduct mileage regardless.

Those who decide to lease must choose between an open-end and a closed-end lease. Most consumer groups recommend the closed-end lease because you assume much less risk when the lease expires.

Whichever car you end up buying, the method you use to finance it or the lease you choose will have a major impact—positively or negatively—on your personal finances. Even though it might require a great deal of concentrated effort to purchase and finance your car, a careful consideration of your options will pay off for years to come.

Using the Internet to Buy Your Car

The online world is revolutionizing car purchasing. If you learn to navigate the Internet as part of your car search, you can probably save yourself hundreds, and possibly thousands, of dollars over the deal you can get by walking into a dealer's showroom and negotiating over the sticker price.

Many of the Web sites listed in Roadmap 5.1 offer car buying services, where you can select, price, and order your car through the Web site. In all of these cases, the Web site works with a member dealer in your vicinity. (Most states in the United States have laws preventing the auto manufacturer from

Roadmap 5.1

Web Sites that Offer Car-Buying Services and Information

American Car Buying Service	http://www.acscorp.com
AutoVantage	http://www.autoadvantage.com
AutoAdvisor.com	http://www.autoadvisor.com
Autobytel.com	http://www.autobytel.com
Autosite	http://www.autosite.com
Autovantage.com	http://www.autovantage.com
AutoWeb	http://www.autoweb.com
Car and Driver	http://www.caranddriver.com
CarBargains	http://www.carbargains.com
Carbuyer.com	http://www.carbuyer.com
CARFAX	http://www.carfax.com
CarInfo.com	http://www.carinfo.com
carlist.com	http://www.carlist.com
Carpoint.	http://www.carpoint.com
CarPrice.com	http://www.carprice.com
CarPrices.com	http://www.carprices.com
CarQ	http://www.carq.com
cars.com	http://www.cars.com
CarsDirect.com	http://www.carsdirect.com
CarSmart.com	http://www.carsmart.com
carsos.com	http://www.carsos.com
ConsumerAuto.com	http://www.consumerauto.com
Consumer Reports.org	http://www.consumerreports.org
DriveOff.com	http://www.driveoff.com
DealerNet.com	http://dealernet.com
edmunds.com	http://www.edmunds.com
giggo.com	http://www.giggo.com
GM BuyPower.	http://www.gmbuypower.com
Insurance Institute for Highway Safety	http://www.highwaysafety.org
IntelliChoice	http://www.intellichoice.com
InvoiceDealers	http://www.invoicedealers.com
Kelley Blue Book	http://www.kbb.com
leasesource	http://www.leasesource.com, http://www.carwizard.com
Lemon-Check	http://www.lemon-check.com
LendingTree	http://www.lendingtree.com
Money.com	http://www.money.com
Motor Trend	http://www.motortrend.com
National Highway Safety Administration	http://www.nhtsa.dot.gov
PeopleFirst.com	http://www.peoplefirst.com
Price Auto Outlet	http://www.priceautooutlet.com
PriceDrive.com	http://www.pricedrive.com
SmartMoney.com	http://www.smartmoney.com/ac/autos/leasing
StoneAge	http://www.stoneage.com
Woman Motorist	http://www.womanmotorist.com

bypassing the dealer and selling the vehicle directly to you.) As a result, you will end up negotiating the best price from the dealer, because in some cases the dealer-quoted price is negotiable and may not be the final price. Most of the Web sites are packed with useful information and can assist you in your selection. And many of them disclose the dealer wholesale cost, which will give you better insight into what the final price should be.

Although the sites disclose the wholesale costs for cars, these prices do not necessarily represent the actual cost to the dealers, because dealer incentives, holdbacks, and bonuses can lower their costs further. In effect, you can conduct a mini-auction online by deciding which car and options you are looking for and requesting quotes from all the sites.

All the major auto manufacturers now have Web sites that may help you get a good deal on a car. For example, General Motors offers the GMBuy-Power service that lets you compare prices on GM cars and other brands and look for your car in dealer inventories. The service also gets dealers to offer you their best prices online. Some sites even offer "virtual test drives" of some of their models.

Other Web sites permit you to assemble the options package that you want online and use this customized package when you ask for bids from dealers. The Web site addresses for carmakers are easy to remember: Most include the name of the manufacturer followed by .com. This makes it easy to find ford.com, gm.com, chrysler.com, toyota.com, and so on. Another way to get all your links to carmakers in one place is by going to this Web site: http://www.carprice.com.You no longer have to settle for the financing package offered by your dealer. Check out http://www.carloan.com or telephone 1-800-CARLOAN to make sure you get the best possible terms from lenders anywhere in the country. As you can see, the Internet can empower you to get the information you need to find the car of your dreams and make sure you get the best price and financing package!

Map Your Future

Saving, Investing, and Finding a Financial Advisor

Some people find it impossible to save money. The problem is legitimate when paying for basics like food, clothing, and shelter takes every penny—and when you're just starting out, these basic expenses may truly take most of your paycheck. Still, there should be *something* left over!

Most people can save if they remove their emotional and psychological roadblocks. All it takes is a change in actions and attitudes. Forget negative thoughts such as, "I'm not smart enough to learn about money," or, "I deserve to buy this now; I don't want to wait." They're an excuse to procrastinate on building your savings.

Fortunately, most limiting thoughts aren't true but result simply from lack of confidence and knowledge. With knowledge comes understanding and the power to make things happen. Small successes give way to big successes, and you begin to save more and more. Eventually, you can save enough to achieve your dreams, whatever they are.

▶ Get on the Savings Highway!

Let's start small to achieve those small successes and learn that you really can do it. Then build up to bigger things. Begin with some basic rules of saving:

1. *Make a realistic budget.* Then work hard to stay within this budget. Occasionally, you can reward yourself with a little something special for making it work. If you haven't already done this, go back to Chapter 1.

2. *Spend less than you earn.* Doing so will create short-term, if not permanent, changes in your lifestyle. Commit to the changes and learn the difference between something you need versus something you want.

3. *Set savings targets.* Create a savings plan (more about this in the next section). Start simply to build your confidence. Determine a realistic amount for a specific time period, and have a goal in mind for your savings.

4. *Make savings automatic.* Arrange for your bank, credit union, and/or mutual fund automatically to deduct a specific amount from your checking account each month. Also, sign up with your employer for automatic payroll deductions.

5. *Think of savings accounts as untouchable except for targeted goals.* Don't use them for anything except true emergencies. Stick to your budget, savings plan, and goals.

According to the Social Security Administration, only 2 to 3 percent of Americans will be financially able to retire at the age of 65 with a comfortable standard of living. What will happen to the remaining 97 to 98 percent? They will be forced to:

▶ reduce their standard of living;

▶ continue working;

▶ rely on other family members; and/or

▶ rely on outside assistance of some sort.

And beyond the lack of financial assets, as we age we should be asking where our retirement income will come from. According to the U.S. Census Bureau, the average yearly income of Americans aged 65 and over is:

▶ below $15,000 for 50 percent of the population

▶ between $15,000 and $35,000 for 32 percent of the population

▶ more than $35,000 for only 18 percent of the population

This information vividly illustrates the need for proper investment planning. Most people want to be able to retire with an income stream near what they were living on while they are working, yet these statistics reveal that most people haven't achieved that goal.

▶ Start Your Trip Early: Estimate the Real Return on Your Investments

Many people just starting out in the financial planning process want to know how long it will take for their savings and investments to grow, as well as how inflation and taxes will affect their money.

Let's begin with three useful concepts that can help you estimate the return on your savings and investments:

1. The "rule of 72"
2. The real rate of return (adjusted for inflation)
3. Tax-adjusted return

The rule of 72 is easy to figure out, but the other two are a bit more complicated, so you may want to check with a financial advisor for help (more on advisors at the end of this chapter).

The rule of 72 is related to that powerful concept of compound interest and is a simple way to tell how long it will take your money to double in value. Simply divide 72 by an interest rate to determine the number of years it will take your money to double. For example, assume you earn a 6 percent real rate of return on your money. How long will it take for $500 to grow to $1,000? 72 ÷ 6 percent = 12 years. Roadmap 6.1 shows how long it will take to double your money, depending on other interest rates that your investment might earn.

Because inflation eats away at your purchasing power, your investments must work hard and smart. The *real return* on your investments is the earnings that *exceed* the rate of inflation. Unfortunately, this means that an investment with a low rate of return actually could have *no* real growth or even *negative* growth after adjusting for inflation and taxes. It can also mean that the after-tax yield on a municipal bond could be higher than that of a corporate bond, even though the corporate bond carries a higher stated rate of return. Smart investors know that it's not what you *make* but what you *keep* that makes the difference. Only after taxes, inflation, and other investment

Roadmap 6.1

Calculating How Long It Takes to Grow Your Savings, at Different Interest Rates

Interest rate	Years to double money
1 percent	72.0
2 percent	36.0
3 percent	24.0
4 percent	18.0
5 percent	14.0
6 percent	12.0
7 percent	10.3
8 percent	9.0
9 percent	8.0
10 percent	7.2
11 percent	6.5
12 percent	6.0
13 percent	5.5
14 percent	5.1
15 percent	4.8

costs have been subtracted can you ascertain your real rate of return. Again, estimating this might require the help of a financial planner.

▶ Increase Your Mileage: Get the Most Money from Your Employer

As discussed in Chapter 3, salary is only part of any total employment offer; benefits are an important piece of a compensation package, and you should consider them carefully before accepting any new position. Fortunately, most large employers and many smaller companies offer benefit packages that include health, disability, and life insurance coverage. When you read your company's benefits package, don't hesitate to ask the benefits administrator if you have any questions. Knowing how benefit programs work can help save money now and in the future.

Often, the greatest advantage of a 401(k) is that many employers contribute to their employees' 401(k) by matching a portion of the money contributed by the employee. For example, for each $100 you contribute to the plan, your employer may add $50 to your account, giving you a total of $150. That's an immediate 50 percent return on your out-of-pocket $100 investment! No tax advantage gives you a better deal. Tollbooth 6.1 shows how to maximize your company's match to your 401(k).

However, if you're earning more than $80,000 a year, be aware of your contribution percentage. If it's too high and you contribute the maximum amount before year-end, you could miss out on a portion of your employer's match. The law allows a maximum annual contribution of $14,000 ($18,000 if age 50 or over) for 2005 and $15,000 ($20,000 if age 50 or over).

Hazard!
Don't Wait: **Now** *Is the Best Time to Save*

To show the value of investing early and the power of compound interest, consider this scenario. Debbie and Tom are fraternal twins and recent high-school graduates. Debbie works part time while attending college and saves $2,000 a year in an Individual Retirement Account. She does this until she is 25 years old, for a total investment of $14,000.

Tom also works and attends school, but he doesn't *start* investing in an IRA until he's 25. Then he faithfully invests $2,000 a year for the next *40* years, for a total investment of $80,000. Both Debbie's and Tom's accounts earn 10 percent per year.

At age 65, Tom has $893,704 and Debbie has $930,641—not a huge difference, but Debbie invested only $14,000, whereas Tom invested $80,000! The value of starting early is obvious, and if Debbie had started investing $2,000 per year at age 14, *her $10,000 investment would be worth $1,174,600 when she turned 65.*

Wherever you are in saving for your future, it's never too late to start—but the sooner, the better. As Albert Einstein said, "Compound interest is the greatest mathematical discovery of all time."

Tollbooth 6.1

Maximizing Your Employer's 401(k) Match

This worksheet can help you determine how much of your salary to contribute to your 401(k) plan to maximize your employer's match.

A. Enter your annual salary.		$_____
B. Enter the number of pay periods.		_____
C. Calculate your pay per period: Divide A by B.	A ÷ B =	$_____
D. Enter your desired annual contribution.		$_____
E. Calculate your contribution per pay period: Divide D by B.	D ÷ B =	$_____
F. Calculate the contribution's percentage of pay: Divide E by C.	E ÷ C =	0._____
G. Multiply F by 100 to determine percentage of pay.	F × 100 =	_____%

Invest as soon as you can after being hired. And consider carefully all your investment options within the plan: choose the mix and type of stocks and bonds you're most comfortable with, to match your risk level. More on this topic in the next section.

▶ Chart Your Journey: Set Financial Goals

Financial planning helps you get from where you are today to where you want to be, and it provides a framework for making related financial decisions. Properly structured, the process helps you evaluate everyday choices and the interrelated financial implications so you can better allocate your resources—personal and financial—to meet your goals, and allows you to move forward with confidence.

Financial planning is about setting personal and financial goals, and then figuring out how to achieve them. It's an ongoing process. Any plan must be reviewed periodically and adjusted if necessary to ensure that it continues to direct you toward your goals.

Dear Sis,

Mom said you're having trouble deciphering your company's 401(k) plan: maybe your big sister can help. My first job had a terrific matching contributions plan: it invested 2 percent of my salary (on top of my salary), and I could invest 5 percent more, which it matched for a total of 12 percent. My co-workers encouraged me to invest the max, but I felt I couldn't: I was having trouble just paying bills. Plus, I was only in my 20s, so retirement seemed so far off! All I invested was 2 percent—big mistake.

When I changed jobs, my new boss told me he'd worked for the same company, and he raved about its retirement plan and how much money he'd saved. I was happy with the $7,000 I'd saved in 3 years— until he said he'd accumulated $67,000! His salary was higher, so his 12 percent was more money than mine; still, I was stunned. I went to HR and immediately filled out the paperwork to invest the maximum amount. That matching contribution was really free money—a true benefit. So please try to set aside the maximum you can: you'll be so much happier when you retire!

Clear the Road: Turn General Ideas into Specific Goals

Establishing personal and financial goals is the first step. Typically, your goals will be general, such as:

► "I want to start my own business."
► "I want to educate my children."
► "I want to retire comfortably."
► "I want to travel and play golf when I retire."

Admittedly, these are *long*-term goals; still, they shouldn't be so vague. These statements don't tell the full story. What exactly do these statements mean to *you*, and what will it take to achieve *your* goal? That's important, because everyone's answer is different. And if you know the financial and personal resources needed to achieve something, you can make sure you're properly allocating and using those resources. After all, you don't want to fall short of realizing your goals later in life. Let's look at a few common goals and how to turn them into measurable action plans that integrate into your financial future.

"I want to start my own business." This goal alone can fill many books. What you need to know, though, is whether you have the strengths, knowledge, skills, interest, and financial resources to achieve this goal. Because so many personal considerations enter into this kind of decision, financial considerations almost take a back seat. But the bottom line once again is to explain clearly what this goal means to you in personal and financial terms so it can be worked into your financial framework.

"I want to be able to educate my children." Does this mean providing every dime to get through college and perhaps graduate school, or just supporting them by cosigning student loans, matching income dollar-for-dollar, or some other way of helping out? Maybe your parents could not afford or chose not to help you with your education costs, and that experience influences how you will help your children. Again, the key is to explain clearly what this goal means to you in personal and financial terms so you can assess the financial impact on your resources.

"I want to retire comfortably." Comfort is the key. What will it take for you to be *comfortable*? How you answer that question determines how much money you need to set aside. Perhaps you want to own your home free and clear and equip it so that you can live there despite any physical challenges. That can require renovations that take financial resources. So for you, *comfortable* may mean setting aside a certain amount of money. But you also have to consider whether your lifestyle will allow you to leave money to your heirs, or whether inflation will require you to tap into those funds. The key is to clearly define your comfort in personal and financial terms so you can model your projected use of money over time. You also need to understand how financial returns and accessibility needs can affect achieving your desires.

Before You Pay Any Tolls: Build Your Savings by Paying Yourself First

Like most people just starting out, you're probably being bombarded with new challenges, commitments, opportunities, and intimidating questions. Making wise financial decisions early in life can have a dramatic effect on your ability to reach your future financial goals. So if you skipped Chapter 1 and haven't already developed a budget, *do it now*. Without a budget and financial plan, it's all too easy for your earnings to wither away.

Manage Your Cash Flow and Debt. Take care of your needs first, then your savings, then the fun stuff. The budget probably will be a bit more difficult to manage than you originally thought, because despite the new source of income, you will have a slew of expenses. An easy way to develop a simple budget is to calculate your monthly cash flow on a simple pad of paper or using a spreadsheet software program like Intuit's Quicken (http://www.quicken.intuit.com), Microsoft Money (http://www.microsoft.com/money), or Mvelopes Personal (http://www.mvelopes.com).

Other budget tips include the following:

▶ Evaluate your spending habits and cut back on nonessentials (as discussed in Chapter 1).

▶ Pay off credit card debt (refer back to Chapter 2).

▶ Recognize that you may no longer be covered under your parents' insurance policy. Don't underestimate the need for adequate insurance, so find out what your company has to offer (refer back to Chapter 3).

Pay Off Your Student Loans. Typically, education loan repayments begin six months after graduation, so don't forget to include them in your initial cash flow worksheet. A few lenders, such as Sallie Mae, offer incentives for borrowers to pay on time or pay electronically. Additionally, interest paid on education loans may be deductible from income taxes if you meet an income test. Income limits, adjusted annually for inflation, are based on a modified version of the borrower's adjusted gross income (AGI). Talk to the IRS or your tax advisor to find out if you meet the income test.

Develop a Savings and Investment Plan. The first step in any financial plan is to ensure that you have an emergency fund with three to six months of living expenses readily available. To calculate how much you need, take your total monthly living expenses, subtract taxes and nonessential expenditures, then multiply the result by a number of months (again, usually three to six). This number is your goal for building a cash reserve.

Start Setting Aside Retirement Savings. Next on the agenda is your retirement savings. It is never too early to begin saving for retirement. Most people say they wished they had started saving earlier—no matter what their age now. Take full advantage of your retirement plan at work, because many employers offer payroll deduction plans where a specified amount is deducted from each paycheck. Put as much as you can into the retirement plan (more on this topic later in this chapter). At a minimum, it should be as much as your employer will match. Some companies, for example, contribute 50 cents for every dollar the employee contributes. That's an immediate 50 percent return on your investment!

Make Your Own Map: Create a Personal Written Plan

This plan will outline exactly where you are today, determine where you need to be in the future, fully explore your personal attitudes toward risk, and outline exactly what rate of return will help you reach your future financial goals. Only with this information can you develop your proper asset allocation.

With your written financial plan, you will be able to determine what amount of your money should be held in cash, what portion should be held in bonds, and what portion should be held in stocks (all of which will be discussed later in this chapter). Each asset class plays a critical role toward moving you closer to financial independence. Yet if you look back at history, it is very difficult to know which blend of assets will be the best for the *future*.

Just Like Learning to Drive: The Basics of Investing and Allocating Your Assets

Asset allocation is the process of determining which asset classes (e.g., stocks, real estate, bonds, cash, and others) you want to include, and in what proportions, in your investment portfolio. It's a critical part of financial planning but often is ignored in favor of sexier stock picking or a broker's hot "tip-du-jour." At its core, asset allocation involves developing a formal investment strategy to achieve your financial objectives. It provides a framework in which to make objective, *unemotional* portfolio decisions. It may not be the way to immediate, exceptional returns, but it is the proven way toward *long-term* wealth accumulation.

Research shows that more than 90 percent of the variation in investment returns among investment portfolios comes from the choice and weighting of asset classes—*not* from which stocks you select or when you buy and sell (known as *market timing*). Asset allocation *de-emphasizes* individual security analysis and selection and instead focuses on how broad asset classes perform and how closely their long-term returns correlate with each other. If the returns of a particular asset class zig when those of others zag, including it in a portfolio can help reduce volatility and improve returns over time.

Figuring out your portfolio's asset allocation depends on your unique circumstances, such as your age, time horizon until retirement (or whenever you're going to want the money you've invested), financial goals, and tolerance for investment risk. Allocation decisions also can be influenced by more transitory factors like market valuations, interest rates, and economic conditions. A portfolio's asset mix will change over time, too, as your circumstances change (for example, if you get married, have children, etc.). So you should review your portfolio's allocation and rebalance it, if necessary, on a regular basis, usually annually. And wherever possible, rebalance with tax consequences in mind.

Taking time now to put together your investment strategy can help you avoid mistakes and move forward with greater confidence. To determine the right portfolio mix for you, start by asking three questions.

1. How long is your investment horizon?
2. What is your tolerance for risk?
3. What are your financial objectives?

How Long Is the Road?
Establishing Your Time Horizon

Your investment time horizon, or when the money will be needed, is important because of the risk or volatility of equities (stocks). Over the longer term, investors generally can assume more risk and thus allocate more of their portfolio to stocks. Roadmap 6.2 shows a potential guideline for an investor's maximum equity exposure.

Here are some common asset allocations for various risk tolerance levels that may serve as an example for you:

Roadmap 6.2

Determining How Much to Invest in Equities

Time Horizon	Maximum Allocation in Equities
0-3 years	0 percent
4-5 years	20 percent
6 years	30 percent
7 years	40 percent
8 years	50 percent
9 years	60 percent
10 years	70 percent
11+ years	80 percent

	STOCKS	BONDS	CASH
Ultraconservative	15 percent	67 percent	18 percent
Fairly Conservative	37 percent	51 percent	12 percent
Moderate	57 percent	38 percent	5 percent
Fairly Aggressive	76 percent	24 percent	0
Ultra-aggressive	93 percent	7 percent	0

These hypothetical illustrations are examples of how various financial portfolios could be allocated among the three basic asset classes. The importance of this information cannot be overemphasized. The single largest factor in the success of your financial plan may be how your personal investments are allocated between cash, bonds, and stocks.

The biggest mistake individual investors make is to put their financial plan into place and then begin to sell assets at the first bond market or stock market downturn. They will often jump out when they should be buying or, at least, holding onto what they have. Structure your investment portfolio so that you are able to sleep at night without being forced to constantly shift assets from one class to another.

How Fast Are You Willing to Go?
Determining Your Tolerance for Risk

Risk tolerance is how you feel and react when the value of your investments declines. For example, suppose you allocated 70 percent of your portfolio to stocks and regularly add to your account. In 2004, you would have watched the bear market take 30 percent of your stocks' value. Can you continue to invest the new dollars needed to maintain your 70 percent allocation to equities, while at the same time watching the value of your portfolio go down?

Over longer periods of time (i.e., 10 to 20 years), history has shown that stocks outperform all other asset classes, so a well-thought-out investment plan can help you stay the course during the market's ups and downs. You want to avoid making emotionally based decisions that will hurt your portfolio's performance over the long run. Roadmap 6.3 offers a guideline to help you determine the right percentage of equity exposure for you based on your risk tolerance.

If you factor the tolerable loss in with the investment time horizon (Roadmap 6.2), the lower of the two percentages should be your portfolio's equity allocation. Defining your personal level of risk tolerance allows you to build a portfolio most suited to helping you reach your future financial goals while allowing you to invest within your comfort zone. Roadmap 6.4 is a short questionnaire that may offer some insight into your personal feelings toward risk. It will also rank some of the common factors that determine your ability to take on risk. These factors include age, income, current savings, and general investment knowledge.

These questions and your score should be used only as a guide because your actual investment plan may vary based on additional information not covered in the questionnaire. But after you have scored your risk tolerance, the next step is creating a portfolio of investments that matches your tolerance for risk.

As you see from the scoring of the questionnaire, you'll find yourself in one of five categories. The asset allocations suggested for each category offer hypothetical examples of the types of allocations available. Your circumstances may change, so you should review your investment allocation periodically and adjust as needed. The investments you select will determine the overall aggressiveness and volatility of your portfolio. Remember that the value of your portfolio will fluctuate with market conditions.

Roadmap 6.3

How Much to Invest in Equities Depending on Your Risk Tolerance

Maximum Tolerable Loss	Maximum Equity Exposure
5 percent	20 percent
10 percent	30 percent
15 percent	40 percent
20 percent	50 percent
25 percent	60 percent
30 percent	70 percent
35 percent	80 percent
40 percent	90 percent
50 percent	100 percent

1. Ultraconservative. As an ultraconservative investor, you prefer income-oriented, guaranteed investments such as CDs and bonds. Your need for income is high and your tolerance for risk is very low. With this in mind, you may wish to consider this sample asset allocation:

Cash	18 percent
Bonds	67 percent
Stocks	15 percent

2. Fairly Conservative. As a fairly conservative investor, you are still uncomfortable with the volatility inherent in the stock market. However, you realize that a long-term commitment to quality growth investments should help you reach your financial goals. Therefore, although you're still primarily interested in fixed income-producing assets, you are willing to increase your allocation to balanced funds and some growth and income funds. If you venture into individual stocks, you are more likely to lean toward large cap, dividend-paying companies. Your basic asset allocation may look like this:

Measuring Your Risk Tolerance

Please circle the number preceding each of your answers.

What is your age?

1 65 and over
3 36-64
5 35 and under

What is your time horizon for investing this money?

1 1 year
2 2-5 years
3 5-10 years
4 10-20 years
5 20 years or longer

What is your primary objective for this money?

1 Safety of principal
2 Current income
3 Growth and income
4 Conservative growth
5 Aggressive growth

Regarding your income, do you expect it to:

1 Decrease dramatically in the future?
2 Decrease a slight amount in the future?
3 Stay about the same?
4 Increase with the pace of inflation?
5 Increase dramatically?

What amount of money do you have set aside for emergencies?

1 None
3 Enough to cover three months of expenses
5 Enough to cover six or more months of expenses

Which statement best describes your personal investment experience?

1 I have never been responsible for investing any money.
2 I am a relatively new investor.
3 I have invested some of my money through IRAs and through
   employer-sponsored retirement plans (401(k)s) for quite some time,
   but now I am ready to develop additional investment strategies.

4 I have invested for quite some time and am fairly confident in my ability to make prudent investment decisions.

5 I have invested money for years and have a definite knowledge of how the various stock and bond markets work.

Regarding your view of risk, which investment would you be more comfortable making?

1 I am comfortable investing in savings accounts and CDs (certificates of deposit) that are FDIC insured.

2 I invest in savings accounts and CDs, but I also own various income-producing bonds and/or bond mutual funds.

3 I have invested in a broad array of stocks, bonds, and mutual funds, but only those of the highest quality.

4 I have invested primarily in growth stocks and growth stock mutual funds.

5 I like to pick out new and emerging growth companies and aggressive growth stock mutual funds.

To understand your risk tolerance more clearly, which investment would you be more likely to invest in?

1 This investment has a 20-year average annual return of 6 percent. It has achieved those returns with infrequent and very slight downturns. This investment has never experienced a negative return.

3 This investment has a 20-year average annual return of 9 percent. It has achieved those returns with a few moderate downturns when the decline lasted less than six months and then began to recover. It has experienced more than one year of negative returns.

5 This investment has a 20-year average annual return of 14 percent. It has achieved those returns while cycling through several periods of above-average returns and several periods of substantially negative returns.

To score the risk tolerance test, simply add up the points. You receive one point for each number that you circled. For example, if you circled a 1, you receive 1 point. If you circled a 4, you receive 4 points. The lowest number of points is 8 and the highest number is 40. Please count the number of points you circled and place a star on the risk tolerance scale below:

Ultra-conservative	Fairly Conservative	Moderate	Fairly Aggressive	Ultra-aggressive
8 10 12 14	16 18 20 22 24 26	28	30 32 34	36 38 40

Cash	12 percent
Bonds	51 percent
Stocks	37 percent

3. Moderate. Moderate investors see themselves as the tortoise in the "Tortoise and the Hare." You are definitely interested in achieving reasonable returns and you have attempted to measure and quantify the risk. You realize there will be periods of negative returns, yet you are determined to commit to a long-term strategy of investing in a variety of growth investments that include large cap stocks, midcap stocks, and even international stocks. However, to reduce the overall volatility of your portfolio, you'll have a healthy portion held in fixed-income assets. Your basic asset allocation would include:

Cash	5 percent
Bonds	38 percent
Stocks	57 percent

4. Fairly Aggressive. As a fairly aggressive investor, you'll be critically aware of the risk-return ratio between your various investment options. You are not at all interested in income, so you spread your money among a variety of more aggressive growth stocks and growth mutual funds. You would be interested in diversifying your money into all the major growth categories (large cap, midcap, small cap, and international). You would want to structure your portfolio to take advantage of growth stock cycles and value stock cycles by owning both types. And because of the higher level of volatility, you'd want to be sure you set a consistent schedule to monitor your progress. Your basic asset allocation might include:

Cash	3 percent
Bonds	21 percent
Equity	76 percent

5. Ultra-aggressive. As an ultra-aggressive investor, you're interested in high return. You are aware of the risks, but you believe in making the most of every dollar. You are interested in investing in growth sectors. You look to new industries for your excitement. However, you are not carried away. You place a considerable portion of your portfolio into large cap and midcap growth stocks. You realize the importance of diversification and know there will be wild swings in the month-to-month value of your accounts. Your basic asset allocation might be:

Cash	0 percent
Bonds	7 percent
Stocks	93 percent

Plan Multiple Routes: Diversify!

To reduce your investing risk, diversify the actual markets in which you are investing your money. As described, begin by deciding what percentage of your assets you want in cash, in bonds, and in stocks. You can also add more asset classes like real estate and precious metals; the most sophisticated investors also look at other commodities and financial futures contracts (often called managed futures). You can thus reduce market risk by diversifying the asset classes in which you invest your money.

You can also reduce some market risk through sector rotation. Though markets often fall in unison, there are usually one or two sectors of the market that do well when other sectors are performing poorly. The stock market can be categorized into the following sectors:

- ▶ Basic materials
- ▶ Energy
- ▶ Technology
- ▶ Health care
- ▶ Consumer cyclicals (Durable)
- ▶ Consumer cyclicals (Nondurable)
- ▶ Consumer noncyclicals
- ▶ Utilities
- ▶ Financials
- ▶ Transportation
- ▶ Telecommunications

You might see a steep decline in basic materials or energy while such sectors as heath care or technology are rebounding.

How Many Miles to the Gallon?
Determining Your Financial Objectives

Finally, what are your financial objectives, and how much potential risk will you likely need to take on to reach them? Sometimes, the amount of money you need drives the amount of risk or equity exposure you will take on. For example, if, based on the number of years to retirement, you need an 8 percent return on your investment, roughly 60 percent of your portfolio should be allocated to equities. But would you still be able to sleep at night while taking this kind of risk with your money?

If the risk to achieve the return is more than you can stomach, but you don't want to reduce your retirement spending plan, the options are to increase your savings or delay your expected retirement date (or some combination of the two) to make up for the lower expected return that comes with taking less risk. The other alternative would be to accept a reduced retirement income. Whatever route you choose, if you develop a good game plan and stick with it, you have the potential to be rewarded.

▶ Which Road to Take? Your Investment Alternatives

The sheer number of investment alternatives that are available to help people reach their goals often overwhelms those just starting out. Many people know they need to invest in order to reach their future goals, but they often lack the confidence to do so. Some people are afraid to ask questions; others may not know how to invest in a stock or mutual fund; still others have questions about various fee structures and associated costs.

The key is to slow down and relax. This is your money. By taking the time to improve your understanding of some of the basic concepts, you will be more informed and more confident about your final decisions.

The three basic asset classes are cash, bonds, and stocks.

An Easy Road: Keeping Your Money in Cash

Cash is wonderful. You can hold it in your hands. You can deposit it in the local bank and make withdrawals at your convenience. You can use it to buy things or pay off debt, or give it away to help people. In addition to physical currency, cash is held in electronic forms. Cash investments include:

- ▶ Paper currency
- ▶ Checking accounts and debit cards
- ▶ Savings and money market accounts
- ▶ Some short-term CDs and bonds with maturities of less than one year

All cash investments are considered short-term investments and are geared to meet short-term needs. For example, you usually keep enough paper currency to buy lunch and fill your car with gas or buy a soft drink at work. You keep enough money in your personal checking accounts to pay your fixed bills and to cover your day-to-day living expenses that you don't pay for with paper currency. You should keep enough money in a savings account or a money market account to cover your emergency fund (most financial planners recommend that you set aside enough money to cover three to six months of expenses). Finally, depending on your age and your personal risk tolerance level, you should plan to keep enough money in short-term CDs or Treasury bills to give you the security your financial plan deserves.

The key to understanding cash investments is that they carry *low risk* and *low return*. They typically have the highest level of safety, but they won't help your money compound at a rapid pace. Inflation is the biggest risk to your cash investments.

So why do people keep cash and other short-term investments? Here are a couple of reasons:

1. *Indecision.* They receive a bonus or accumulate an extra amount of money in their cash accounts, and because of an inability to make a decision, they leave the money in a low-yielding cash account.
2. *Lack of knowledge.* They have done an excellent job of accumulating the money, but they have never learned what to do next.

All of us need to have some money invested in cash. But your cash investments should be used for what they were intended to do. They should be used to provide necessary liquidity; they should be used for your emergency fund; and they should be used by risk-averse investors as a percentage of their overall financial plan.

A Gentle Road: Investing in Bonds

The second basic asset class is bonds. Bonds are often considered boring and that is exactly what makes them so attractive. You put $10,000 into a 10-year U.S. government bond; for 10 years your semiannual income checks arrive like clockwork; and at the end of the ten years, you get your $10,000 back. Not a lot of guesswork, few surprises—you buy your bonds and live on or reinvest the income.

How Bonds Work. Let's look at how an actual bond investment might work. Assume that XYZ Corporation wants to build a new manufacturing plant. This company has been in business for more than 50 years and carries the highest-quality investment ranking. Now it needs to raise $100 million to pay for the new plant and equipment. Where does it find that kind of money? From investors just like you.

Suppose you have $10,000 to invest and XYZ Corporation is issuing a new $100 million bond to build a new plant. These bonds carry the highest-quality rating and will pay 6 percent interest for 10 years. Because corporate bonds don't carry FDIC insurance as a certificate of deposit does and the bond has a 10-year maturity, the 6 percent income yield is appealing. So investors like you invest in this bond issue, thus providing XYZ Corporation the capital it needs to build a new plant. Tollbooth 6.2 shows how you make money from this bond.

Quality bonds are considered less volatile than stocks and are thought to provide a steady income stream. Bonds give you the opportunity to put a specific amount of money into an investment, receive a specific and usually dependable return, and then get your original investment back on a specific future date.

   Tollbooth 6.2

Money Earned on a 10-year $10,000 Bond

The XYZ bond might look like this after you make
a $10,000 principal investment:

2005	$600 interest, paid as $300 payments semiannually
2006	$600 interest
2007	$600 interest
2008	$600 interest
2009	$600 interest
2010	$600 interest
2011	$600 interest
2012	$600 interest
2013	$600 interest
2014	$600 interest plus your original $10,000 principal to be repaid on the stated maturity date

Bond Basics. Regardless of the type of bond or fixed-income instrument you purchase, it will tend to have certain common features:

▶ Corporate and government bonds trade in $1,000 increments.
▶ Municipal bonds trade in $5,000 increments.
▶ Bonds have a "face value" or "par value" or "maturity value," which is what the bonds are expected to be worth when they mature.
▶ They have a stated maturity date ranging from a few days to 30 to 40 years.
▶ They have a stated interest rate, which is the percentage they are expected to pay based on the face value of the bond.
▶ They may be rated by one of the rating services; Standard and Poor's and Moody's are two of the major ones. These services assign a letter rating based on the following scale:

	S&P	MOODY'S
Highest Quality	AAA	Aaa
	AA	Aa
	A	A
	BBB	Baa
	BB	Ba
Lower Quality	B	B

The ratings continue, but AAA through BBB are considered "investment grade bonds" with AAA being the highest quality and moving on to higher-risk and higher-yield bonds.

Most bonds pay semiannual interest, except for Treasury bills, which pay interest at maturity, and zero-coupon bonds, which work like savings bonds and are purchased at a discount and grow in value until maturity.

The most difficult concept for investors to grasp is that while bonds are often issued and originally purchased at a round number like $10,000, they quickly begin to trade at different prices in the open market. For example, suppose you bought the $10,000 XYZ bond described earlier. XYZ stated it would pay you 6 percent interest for 10 years. What happens to the value of that investment if interest rates rise and within 2 years a similar bond could be purchased with an 8 percent yield?

Who would want to buy your 6 percent bond when they could buy an 8 percent bond? No one would buy it for the full value of $10,000 that you paid, but someone would offer to buy it from you at a discount that would give them a yield equivalent to the 8 percent. So if you needed to sell your 6 percent bond, someone might offer to pay you $8,640.97, which could result in a $1,359.03 principal loss if you needed to sell it. Many investors look at the income stream alone and don't realize that bonds actually move up and down in value based on the interest rate movements that are occurring in the economy.

Although you don't need to know all of the ins and outs of how bond prices function, it is helpful to know some of the basics:

▶ Bond prices move inversely to interest rates.
▶ As interest rates move higher, bond prices fall.
▶ As interest rates move lower, bond prices rise.

There are also various bond strategies:

1. Buying short-term bonds—i.e., less than 5 years. Short-term bonds will carry the lowest yields and the smallest amount of principal fluctuation. Risk averse investors often buy high-quality short-term bonds.

2. Buying intermediate-term bonds—i.e., 5 to 10 years. These bonds should give you a somewhat higher yield than a similar quality short-term bond, but because of their extended maturity dates, they have more volatile price fluctuations. Investors hoping to capture a higher income may buy intermediate bonds. You might also buy intermediate bonds if you thought interest rates were going to remain the same or decline in the future.

3. Buying long-term bonds—i.e., 10 to 30 years. They often pay an even higher rate of return than an intermediate bond, but because of their length, they have the most price volatility. You would be interested in long-term bonds if you felt sure that interest rates would be declining or if you simply wanted the higher income.

4. "Laddering"—i.e., investing in bonds that will mature at different times: for example, if you have $100,000 to invest in the bond portion of your asset allocation, you would choose the type and quality of bond that you wish to invest in and then stagger, or ladder, the maturity dates by placing $10,000 into each bond. This is a practical strategy because it's impossible to predict which way interest rates will move.

5. Buying "zero-coupon" bonds—i.e., bonds that pay no interest; instead, they are offered to investors at a discount with a specific maturity date

when they will grow to their full face value. For example, a 10-year zero-coupon Treasury note purchased today might have a face value of $10,000. Your purchase cost would be approximately $6,000. At that price this bond would have a yield to maturity of roughly 5.25 percent. Zero-coupon bonds are often used to prefund specific investment goals such as a child's college education or personal retirement. Zero-coupon bonds can be purchased as Treasury bonds, corporate bonds, or tax-free municipal bonds. They offer a wonderful method of investing money without having to wonder what your rate of return will be. On the other hand, a disadvantage is that they generate taxable income every year if they are purchased in your personal account, and long-term zeros have a higher degree of volatility and their rate of return is low.

The Riskiest, Rockiest Road: Investing in Stocks

Stocks have historically provided the highest rates of investment return of all the major asset classes. By definition, stocks are equity ownership in a publicly traded company. That ownership is typically represented as shares of stock, and these shares can be physically issued in certificate form (though this is rare today) or they can be held in book entry form at your financial institution.

When you buy stock, you have the opportunity to share in the profits of the company, but you also share in the company's risk of losses. Stocks are very different from bonds in that they don't have to pay you anything. Remember, bonds have a written obligation to pay an investor interest. Stocks are under no obligation to pay any dividends or any other form of compensation. Although many companies *choose* to pay their shareholders dividends, those income payments are set once a quarter and may be changed or eliminated at the discretion of the board of directors.

Large Cap, Midcap, and Small Cap Stocks. There are three major classes of common stock: large capitalization, midcapitalization, and small capitalization stocks, better known in their abbreviated forms. But the type of stock that falls into each category and the risk-return ratio of each group varies greatly:

1. *Large cap stocks* refer to companies with a market capitalization over $2 billion. These are often well-known names and are usually referred to as blue chip stocks.

2. *Midcap stocks* refer to companies with a market capitalization from $500 million to $2 billion. These are usually not as well known but may offer a more aggressive growth potential.

3. *Small cap stocks* refer to companies with a market capitalization of less than $500 million. They are less likely to be known by the average investor, but history (since 1926) has shown that over time they have generated the largest returns.

The importance of understanding the capitalization of each stock or mutual fund that you select is that each of these broad categories will come in and out of favor.

How can you choose an appropriate blend to help you meet your future financial goals? Only after a detailed review of your current assets, your stated goals and objectives, and your level of risk tolerance can you or your financial professional structure a portfolio designed to meet your goals.

One final distinction must be made within the types of stocks (or stock mutual funds) you choose to hold, between value stocks and growth stocks:

1. A *value* stock is typically characterized by market sectors often thought of as dull, such as paper stocks, chemical stocks, and autos. It is often thought that a savvy investor will attempt to buy these companies when they are out of favor and wait patiently for the markets to recognize their true value. Some common large cap value stocks include DuPont, Eastman Kodak, Burlington Northern, Alcoa, and Sears.

2. The opposite of value investing is *growth* investing. A company may be considered a growth stock if it has a projected earnings per share growth rate of 15 to 50 percent per year. During the dot-com boom, Internet stocks and most large technology companies fell into this category. Other sectors include drug companies, consumer companies, and some large multinational companies.

You may now think you need to own some stocks—with the returns that have been generated over the past 15 years, you may be thinking of putting a large portion of your money into stocks. But there is a catch: not all stocks go up in value. There are many companies whose value may rise quickly, only to have their product or service become obsolete. Sometimes high-quality stocks can have slow growth periods and the slower-than-expected earnings growth can affect the stock's price. And sometimes the overall market will decline—even if your stock holdings are continuing to show outstanding earnings growth, the overall tone of the market can force a broad stock decline.

Assessing the Value of a Stock. Many factors impact the value of a stock, as explained in the following paragraphs.

1. *EPS—earnings per share.* This is the net income divided by the number of shares outstanding. For example, if a company earned $1 million and has 1 million shares of stock outstanding, then this company would report an earnings per share of $1. Determining EPS is the most frequently used method of monitoring whether a company is making money and growing at a reasonable rate. Most long-term investors are looking to buy stock in companies that have had a long history of steady and increasing earnings per share. Investors want to believe that their companies will continue to have similar or better growth potential in the future.

2. *Stable management teams.* Many analysts and investors look for companies that have had the same management teams in place for a long time. Also, investors like to see that members of senior management personally own a large stake of common stock in the company they are running. Abrupt changes in senior management can cause investors to lose confidence in a company.

3. *Future growth prospects.* Is the company in a growing industry that has a tremendous amount of upside potential? Or is it in a more mature industry whose growth is slowing but is more assured?

4. *Unforeseen surprises.* The stock market reacts very strongly to unforeseen surprises, both on the upside and the downside. The price of a stock can jump sharply over the release of a new product or service or a potential merger or acquisition. But prices can drop just as quickly if a company reports any negative news. And stock prices can be impacted by more than a company's business plan and its future. When the overall stock market becomes jittery or overvalued, many stocks may decline in anticipation of a slowing economy or an unexpected rise in short-term interest rates.

There are many things that affect stock prices, but the bottom line is this: If people are rushing to buy into the stock of a company, those shares will be rising. And if people are rushing to sell out of the stock of a company, those shares will be falling. It is a matter of supply and demand.

How you buy stock. Stocks are traded on public exchanges. Some of the larger exchanges include the New York Stock Exchange, the recently merged American Stock Exchange, and the Nasdaq (National Association of Security Dealers Automated Quotes).

First, determine which stock you want to buy. Next, look up the ticker symbol, which is usually a two-, three- or four-letter symbol used to access the computer information regarding every major publicly traded stock. For example, General Motors' ticker symbol is GM (though not all ticker symbols are obvious abbreviations). Once you know the ticker symbol, you can find out the current market value of the stock. There will always be two prices, a bid price and an asked price. The *bid price* is what an investor is willing to pay for the stock—e.g., $12 per share; the *asked price* is what a seller is willing to sell the stock for—e.g., $11 per share. You might also meet in the middle at $11.50 per share, or possibly no transaction will be made if you can't agree on a price. The prices of most stocks are constantly moving during the hours of the open market. The price of each security is determined primarily by supply and demand. When a lot of people want to buy the stock and only a few are willing to sell, the stock price will move up. If a lot of people want to sell their shares of stock and no one is there to buy, the share value will drop.

You should also be aware of the two most common types of orders: *market orders* and *limit orders.* A market order is by far the most common; it most likely assures you of an execution of your trade. A market order states that you are willing to pay whatever the market requires to fill your order. If you are a buyer, you are willing to take the seller's price; if you are a seller, you are willing to accept the buyer's price.

However, if you are afraid the market could move sharply, you could place a limit order and say, "I want to buy 100 shares of GM, but only if I can buy it at no more than $14." A limit order allows you to specify the target price at which you want to buy or sell your stock. A limit order can help protect you from skyrocketing IPOs (initial public offerings) that you may wish to purchase.

Once you have determined the type of order, decide exactly how much money you want to invest. After looking up the most recent dollar price of the stock in a newspaper or on the Internet, you can determine how many shares you are able to purchase. You often hear financial professionals discuss buying in increments of 100 shares, which are considered "round lots" and are often used as the recommended increments (100 shares, 200 shares, etc.). However, you may purchase stock in any increment, even as few as one share at a time. Most financial professionals wouldn't recommend buying one share at a time because of the higher transaction costs to you and the issuing company. After purchasing your shares, you usually have three days to pay for your stock. This is called the settlement date, and you are required to pay for your purchase on or before that date. Some investment companies may require you to deposit money before a trade is made, especially if you plan to purchase any of the more volatile technology or Internet companies.

As an owner of shares, you can immediately begin to participate in the movements in the price of the shares; and you begin to receive the company's annual and quarterly reports. Whether you are purchasing your first stock or your hundredth, researching the companies, evaluating their potential, and physically placing your investment money on the line and becoming an owner of a corporation is almost always an exciting event. The expectation of profit and the intrigue of being involved in some of the fastest-growing corporations in the world can be a rewarding experience.

At a Crossroad: Assessing the Three Asset Classes

Now that you know something about various investing alternatives, here's a quick overview of when you might want to buy one or the other.

Cash and Other Short-Term Investments. Invest in cash if:

► You want short-term investments to meet short-term needs.
► You want to hold cash and cash equivalents for your emergency funds.
► You believe interest rates will be moving higher and you don't want to lock your other fixed-income investments into longer-term maturities.
► You believe the stock market is too high and could fall in the near future.

Bonds and Other Fixed Income Investments. Invest in bonds if:

► You want to generate the steady income stream and reduced volatility of bonds.
► You believe interest rates will be moving higher: then invest in shorter-term bonds.
► You believe interest rates will be moving lower: then invest in longer-term bonds.

- ▶ You are uncertain as to which direction interest rates may be moving: then invest in a laddered-bond portfolio.
- ▶ You don't need the income but still like the idea of receiving a specific amount of money on a specific maturity date: then invest in zero-coupon bonds.

Stocks and Other Growth Investments. Invest in stocks if:

- ▶ You believe inflation could be a risk for your future purchasing power.
- ▶ You believe that corporations will continue to have an increasing earnings stream.
- ▶ You want to profit from the creation and sale of goods and services in the U.S. and around the world.
- ▶ You want to take advantage of the risk-return opportunity in a growing economy (but if you see a slowing economy and/or rising interest rates, then you may want to lower your allocation in stocks). Unfortunately, we never know when interest rates will be rising or when the economy will be slowing.

Which Road to Take? Other Investing Options

Many people just starting out obviously don't have a lot of money to invest, so they don't meet the account minimums set by many brokerages and investment firms. Nevertheless, options abound for starting an investment program with limited funds (usually less than $1,000). Here are just a few:

Direct Stock Purchases and DRIPS. These are an excellent method to invest in individual stocks with little up-front money. More than 1,200 companies allow small, monthly purchases of their stock directly with no commission costs. In addition, your dividends can be reinvested without charge. You can call the Direct Stock Purchase Plan Clearinghouse (800-774-4117) or visit its Web site (http://www.dripinvestor.com) for more information. The primary disadvantage of direct stock purchase plans, however, is the lack of diversity in your portfolio; so be sure to diversify your holdings in other ways.

Mutual Funds. Mutual funds are pooled investments that can provide instant diversification. Many fund companies also offer low-cost investing; however, most funds have minimum initial purchase requirements of $500 to $1,000 and up. Those minimums usually are lower for shares purchased for your IRA ($250 and up) or through automatic investment plans ($25 a month and up). Here are a few sources to help you find low-cost mutual funds include the following:

► *Money* magazine (http://www.moneymag.com). Use the search tool, then click on Mutual Funds.
► Mutual Funds *Investors Center* (http://www.mfea.com). You can screen for "funds for less than $50."

Discount Brokerages. Specialized low-cost discount brokerages offer another option for starting with less than $100. Two such companies are ShareBuilder (www.sharebuilder.com) and BUYandHOLD (http://www.buyandhold.com). Most discount brokerages have lots of options for mutual fund investors, including No-Transaction-Fee (NTF) funds. Keep in mind, though, that the fees to purchase mutual funds that are not part of the broker's NTF program often range from about $15 per trade to more than $100, depending on the size of the investment. One company that has no transaction fees, provides access to all the funds on its platform, and charges a minimal annual custodial fee is FTJ Fund Choice (http://www.ftjfundchoice.com).

Although you may feel as if investing little bits of money is not worth the bother, doing so, carefully and over time, can add up, as shown in this chapter (recall the Hazard Sign about the advantages of compound interest). Everyone must start somewhere, so get started now!

► How's Your Driving? Evaluating the Performance of Your Investments

Successful investing requires an evaluation of the performance of your investments every six to twelve months. You should do this to make sure your investment strategy is on track. Too often this evaluation boils down to a simple, "If my portfolio is up, then I'm doing well, and if it's down, then I'm disappointed." A more reliable, objective way to measure your returns is to use benchmarks.

In the language of investing, a benchmark has come to mean an index or average against which a group of other securities can be compared. An *index,* then, is usually a group of individual securities that have been selected to stand as a proxy for a whole category of securities (for instance, international securities or large-cap domestic).

The idea to use an index as a benchmark is not new. In fact, it was for this purpose that Charles Dow developed the Dow Jones Industrial Average (DJIA) in 1896. At that time, what has become the DJIA was composed of 12 of the biggest companies in the United States. Today, it includes 30 of the largest and most influential blue-chip companies in the country and is the most widely recognized financial index in the world. You will often hear it referred to as "the market" in the media. Although it's well known, the Dow Jones has a shortcoming because it includes only 30 of the thousands of public companies in America.

Therefore, the Standard and Poor's 500 Index (also referred to as the S&P 500) has become more popular as the benchmark of choice for the U.S. stock market. It includes the 500 most widely held companies and covers *all major industries* in the economy—including transportation and utilities, which are absent from the DJIA. Its 500 companies represent about 70 percent of the U.S. market, and its performance is considered to be a solid barometer of overall market performance.

The growing interest in technology and other high-growth companies has resulted in more attention for The Nasdaq Composite Index, which was created in 1971. Unlike the DJIA or the S&P 500, this index includes all of the more than 4,000 companies that trade on the Nasdaq exchange. Because these companies tend to be more speculative and risky, the index tends to be more volatile than the other broad indexes.

Although these three indexes may be the best known and most widely followed, there are many others: for example, The Wilshire 5000 and the Russell 2000. The Wilshire 5000 (which despite its name contains over 6,500 stocks traded in the United States) is sometimes considered a "total market index." The Russell 2000, on the other hand, focuses on small-cap companies and thus includes only those firms with market capitalizations of no more than $550 million. There are others: Foreign and regional stock indexes, sector indexes, and more, lots more.

In addition, you can simplify your plan by investing in index funds. These are mutual funds that have been designed to mimic the performance of an asset class. For example, if you want to invest in large-cap U.S. stocks, instead of picking individual companies, you can buy an index mutual fund that holds the same stocks as the S&P 500.

So here's a recap of what you should have done already and what you need to do next to check out how well your financial portfolio is performing:

1. Determine your long-term financial goals, such as paying for a college education for your kids, or funding your retirement.
2. Carefully evaluate your tolerance for risk.
3. Allocate your assets.
4. Identify an index that has a close correlation to each asset class of your investment portfolio.
5. Assume that the best you will do over time is what the market does over the same period. Remember that 80 percent of the efforts to beat the market fail.
6. At least once a year, measure the returns on your portfolio against those of the index that most accurately reflects its components. If the performance is as good as or better than the benchmark, you are on track. If the performance falls short of the benchmark, consider changing the investments that correspond to that asset class.

Hazard!
Mistakes to Avoid

Be careful not to use a benchmark that does not correlate to a particular asset class in your portfolio. Using a small-cap index such as the Russell 2000 to assess your returns from a portfolio comprised of the large-cap stocks—or a large-cap balanced mutual fund—will tell you little and will likely mislead you because the historical performance of large-cap stocks is quite different from that of small-cap stocks. Instead, measure this group of large-cap value and growth stocks against the S&P 500 Index.

Also, watch the highs and the lows of the markets. If your mid-cap value fund is returning 9.3 percent over the past 12 months, but your mid-cap value benchmark is up 11.1 percent, it is not time for you to be celebrating. You may want to make a change if the returns of your mid-cap assets keep lagging behind the benchmark. Conversely, if your mid-cap value fund is returning 17.1 percent over the past 12 months, and you mid-cap value benchmark is only up 5.1 percent, you should check the underlying sectors and industries that the mutual fund manager is investing in. Over-performance like this is usually due to what is called *style drifting*—which, in this case, may mean that the manager could be investing in growth stocks—something you may or may not want in your portfolio at that time and in that weighting.

If You're Lost and Need a Map: Where to Find Information

Most major metropolitan newspapers have a finance section where they publish daily, quarterly, and/or year-to-date index performance. *USA Today, The Wall Street Journal, Barron's, Investors' Business Daily,* and other financial dailies are also a good resource.

In addition, here are some Web sites you may wish to visit for benchmark information:

- ▶ http://www.factset.com/www_23.asp
- ▶ http://www.morningstar.com
- ▶ http://www.lipperweb.com/daily.shtml
- ▶ http://www.russell.com/ww/indexes/default.asp

▶ Finding a "Tour Guide": Working with a Financial Planner

If you don't feel up to the task of creating a financial plan for yourself, don't worry: there are plenty of resources out there to help you. But you want to find a planner who is right for *you* and will look out for *your* best interests. Education and experience are important, but a financial planner who looks great on paper still may not be right for you. You need to ask specific questions and be prepared to understand the answers you receive. Also, amazingly, people are embarrassed to ask an advisor how and how much they get paid. Don't be. It's your money, so look for the best value in everything you buy, including financial advice.

Get a Map: Seek Out the Expertise You Need

Look for an advisor who maintains a thorough knowledge of the financial issues important to you. If you need an overview of your entire financial situation, consider working with an advisor who has earned the CFP® professional marks of distinction. Also, look for someone experienced in working with people in your situation, and who truly wants to work with and help you. Although many financial advisors focus on serving the wealthy and therefore impose minimum income levels, investment assets, or annual fees, a growing number of qualified advisors can and will work with people who are just starting out on an independent, commission-free basis.

Many people may be qualified to help you evaluate your financial situation. Now is the time to learn how to determine which type of advisor will most closely suit your personal needs.

Certified Financial Planner. This is someone who has taken several training courses to gain the knowledge and expertise to design written financial plans for clients; these courses include:

▶ Financial planning and insurance
▶ Investment planning
▶ Income tax planning
▶ Retirement planning and employee benefits
▶ Estate planning

Each of these courses teaches certified financial planners both skills and ethics. A certified financial planner carries the designation CFP, which assures clients that the planner has fulfilled the necessary requirements and has kept up sufficiently with his or her continuing education to be able to offer clients a high level of service and professionalism.

For these services, a customer may pay a fee or may pay commissions. Before you agree to the services offered by a certified financial planner, you should have the CFP fully outline all fees and costs.

Financial Advisor or Stockbroker. An advisor or broker may also be a fully licensed and trained financial executive. He or she may work for a major national or regional company, or for an independent investment company. While working for one of these companies, most financial advisors are given ongoing training, having already passed the Series 7 examination. This training and testing should mean that your stockbroker can help you create and maintain a financial plan for your family. However, because different financial advisors often focus on different aspects of investing, you may wish to see samples of financial plans and ask how fees are determined. By seeing the type of work different brokers/advisors perform, you should be better equipped to make an informed decision. Your job is to find a financial advisor whose long-term strategies and values conform with yours.

Tax Advisor or CPA. A tax advisor or CPA may also be an excellent source of information for your financial planning process. In many cases, it is advisable to take a team approach. You may wish to hire a financial advisor and a CPA or tax attorney to work together as a team to prepare and/or review the working financial plan. Remember that taxes play a role in your financial planning process, and although they should not be the only factor in your financial decisions, it is good to study their impact. Here are some of the differences and similarities between the various advisors:

CERTIFIED FINANCIAL PLANNER	FINANCIAL ADVISOR/ STOCKBROKER	TAX ADVISOR/CPA
Fee Based and/or Commission Based	*Fee Based and/or Commission Based*	*Fee Based*
Gathers data and establishes goals	Should gather data; establishes goals	Should gather data; establishes goals
Evaluates information and recommends a plan	Evaluates information and recommends a plan	Evaluates information
Implements the plan	Implements the plan	Depends on qualifications and licenses of the person
Monitors the plan	Monitors the plan	Monitors the plan
		May consider tax impact/prepare returns

Whether you choose a fee-based financial planner, a financial advisor, or a CPA, you may wish to interview several of these professionals to compare and contrast their strengths. It is also important to compare and contrast the costs associated with each type of planner. The bottom line: Will they get you where you need to go?

How will your advisor evaluate the information? Many financial advisors in today's environment use a wide assortment of computer software. Therefore, your advisor's plan will probably include some or all of the following:

► A written policy statement outlining the parameters of your goals and objectives
► A clear statement of your risk tolerance level
► A review of your budget
► A list of your current financial assets and current asset allocation
► Help in quantifying your specific goals and guidance on how to reach those goals

► A review of your estate plan (if you have one) and insurance
► Specific recommendations regarding how much money you should be investing on a regular basis to reach your written goals
► Recommendations for any changes in your current holdings and for specific investments to match your risk tolerance level while allowing you to maximize your rates of return within your risk constraints

Understand the Map: Evaluate the Services Offered by Each Financial Planner

One way financial planners differentiate themselves is in how they package and deliver services. Most veteran advisors prefer to work with clients on an ongoing basis. They target clients needing comprehensive financial planning advice and investment management services, meet with them two to four times per year, and may charge annual retainer fees (which can be substantial). Clients who opt for an ongoing retainer relationship are referred to as *delegator-type* individuals.

Other planners have begun to work with their clients on an hourly, as-needed basis. Clients who want advice only when they request it, are known as *validators* or do-it-yourselfers. Although the annual retainer-fee scenario may be effective for clients who need or want to turn over the management of their financial affairs to an advisor, many people cannot afford or justify the ongoing fees. To determine which type of working relationship is right for you, ask yourself if you want periodic input to or validation of your financial decisions or full-time financial management. The cost difference is significant, so don't pay for more service and advice than you need. Making mistakes with your personal finances is the most expensive lesson you will ever learn. When you need professional guidance, seek it out and be willing to pay for it.

Tolls Vary! So Consider Compensation

Don't be afraid to ask how an advisor is compensated and by whom. It's imperative that you are aware of how that compensation may affect your relationship with the advisor and the recommendations you receive. Financial planners and consultants, investment advisors, registered representatives, insurance agents, stock brokers, and bank representatives may all be compensated via commissions and/or fees, and often both. Additional information and a series of charts that allow you to compare planners' compensation

across various service models and portfolio amounts can be found at www.
garrettplanning.com. The following sections describe different types.

Commission-compensated advisors. The oldest and most common form of
compensation is commissions earned on the sale of insurance and investment
products. Though many honest, qualified advisors earn a majority of their
income from commissions, conflicts of interest may arise. These people are
paid for recommending and selling products from companies that, in turn,
pay them commissions. Consciously or unconsciously, that may influence
their recommendations.

It's also important to understand that commissions, fees, and loads generally are not charged as a separate line item; instead they are hidden or ab-
sorbed into the investment. If you don't normally write a separate check to
compensate the advisor, it may seem as if the advice you are getting is free.
Of course, it's not, nor should it be. Note: The term *fee-based* is synonymous
with *fee plus commission.*

Salaried financial advisors. If a planner is a salaried employee of a bank, financial firm, or discount broker, they have much less potential compensation
conflict. Still, you should always ask about sales quotas, incentives (such as
bonuses or vacations), or directives to recommend certain financial products
over others. Salaries often depend on an advisor's ability to meet sales quotas;
and quotas, incentives, and directives can lead to divided loyalties.

Fee-only advisors. Fee-only financial advisors are compensated exclusively
by fees paid directly by you, the client. They do not accept commissions or
compensation from any source other than their clients. A client writes a
check or receives an invoice for the amount to be withdrawn from their investment account to pay the fee. The costs of the advisor's services are very
clear. Consequently, the vast majority of inherent conflicts of interest regarding compensation are removed from this arrangement.

Fee-only wealth managers. Comprehensive, fee-only advisors traditionally
charge a flat fee for the initial comprehensive financial plan, then charge an
annual retainer or a percentage of the assets for which they provide ongoing
financial management services. Fees for comprehensive financial planning
and asset management typically range from 1 to 2 percent per year on a total
investment portfolio. The management fee is debited from the investment
account, usually on a quarterly basis.

The bottom line is that these advisors attempt to set fee schedules and minimums to compensate themselves fairly for their time and expertise. Ask yourself, however, if you need all they provide on an ongoing basis. You may be paying for and receiving more than you really need.

Another consideration with asset management arrangements is that planners may tell you they're on your side because of the financial incentive to help your portfolio perform well. In theory this sounds good, but you need to make sure you are not taking on more risk than you want simply to make a higher short-term return on your investment portfolio.

If you're thinking about turning over management of your financial affairs to another person, you owe it to yourself to do your homework.

Hourly, fee-only advisors. If you want to maintain an active role in and more control over your financial affairs, or if you don't have the big portfolio required by some firms (the typical account minimum for fee-only asset management is $250,000 or more), hourly, fee only advisors are a good option. Such advisors can provide competent, affordable advice.

Fortunately, many advisors offer their services for a flat amount by the project or the hour. This opens the door to one-time meetings, financial checkups, and the opportunity to get a second opinion before a big financial decision. It also works if you want to develop a long-term relationship, because all charges are on the table and can be contracted on an as-needed basis. The reality is that most people probably don't need or want a full-time financial advisor but would truly benefit from meeting with a planner from time to time. Being able to do so on an hourly, as-needed basis puts you in the driver's seat, letting you determine the scope of engagement.

Ask for Directions: Interview Prospective Financial Planners

Creating and implementing a financial plan is a lifelong process, so you want to find someone you will enjoy working with over a long period of time. You may hit it off from the moment you meet, or it may take some time to develop a sense of confidence. You want someone who has integrity and is trustworthy, helpful, courteous, responsive, caring, intelligent, proactive, and more.

The first meeting with a prospective financial advisor will possibly be the most telling one of all. New clients typically decide whether they will do business with a specific financial advisor within the first few seconds of their meeting. First impressions do make a difference, and you should feel at ease with your advisor from the very start. If you're nervous, though, that's perfectly understandable. Money is a very personal and private matter. Right or wrong, it contributes to our feeling of self-esteem. Money does indeed carry very powerful emotions.

When interviewing a prospective advisor, your job is to ask certain important questions. Here are a few examples:

▶ What type of services and products do you specialize in?
▶ Do you hold any special investment planning credentials?
▶ Are you capable of helping me create a written financial plan?
▶ How will you correspond with me? Telephone? Mail? Annual or semi-annual meetings?
▶ What are the costs?
▶ How do you get paid?
▶ Do you like working with investors like me?
▶ Would you be willing to create a written proposal for my review without any obligation?

In turn, the planner might ask you some or all of the following questions:

▶ What does your money mean to you?
▶ What are you planning for?
▶ What are your expectations for your money?
▶ What would your expectations of me include?

A more detailed list of questions is available on the National Association of Personal Financial Advisors' Web site (http://www.napfa.org). Download their brochure, "How to Choose a Financial Planner," and their interview questionnaire, or use The Garrett Planning Network's "Advisor Interview Questionnaire" (see http://www.GarrettPlanningNetwork.com). Be sure to complete a questionnaire for every planner you interview.

Start your quest by visiting the advisor's Web site. Hopefully, the site will answer many of your questions. An independent advisor's site often won't be as flashy as that of a big company, but ask yourself how much of the big company's content directly applies to the advisor you're interviewing. Don't be fooled by glitzy, grand Web sites. Also, be wary of advisors whose sites require you to divulge personal information and/or contact information as a prerequisite for access to the information pertinent to prospective clients.

When you find one or more advisors who appear to meet your primary requirements, call them. If you're comfortable in the initial few minutes of the call, ask to meet in person. Beware of the advisor who wants to meet right away unless you have indicated that it's an emergency. That advisor may be too new, too desperate, or too pushy. Most financial planners and advisors will offer a free initial interview or get-acquainted session. Based on the complexity of your situation and scope of services needed, these meetings can last 45 to 90 minutes. In the meeting, be sure to address the issues that are most important to you first. This will save time for both of you.

The initial interview should provide the following:

► Answers to all the questions on your Interview Questionnaire
► A written proposal or contract that outlines the services the advisor recommends and how, when, and how much they will be compensated
► A list of financial documents and data needed to perform the analysis and provide advice
► A target time frame for when the services could be rendered
► An appreciation for the advisor's professional style and communication and listening skills

Under no circumstances should you start working with an advisor until you're satisfied with the interview process, the recommended services, and the method and amount of compensation. *Don't let anyone pressure you*, but understand that it's the advisor's responsibility to help you take actions they think are in *your best interest.*

You also may want to ask the planner how they define success with a client. If the response is "an expected rate of return on the investment portfolio," that tells you the advisor may focus primarily on investments and total return. It's an easily measured yardstick, but at what cost? Did they take unnecessary risks with your investments because the rate of return goal was not appropriate for you?

On the other hand, if the advisor defines success "based on the client's achievement of his or her financial objectives," that tells you that they approach client relationships with a holistic or comprehensive view. Many of the benefits of financial planning are intangible. The holistic financial advisor may define success as achieving clients' peace of mind, securing their retirement, or helping them realize their dreams.

Consider asking the advisor for referrals from other clients or peer professionals, and interview those people as well. But keep in mind, advisors will select people who will say good things about them. If you ask the right questions and hear the right answers, you are more likely to end up with the right planner for you.

Additional information and a series of charts that allow you to compare planners' compensation across various service models and portfolio amounts can be found at http://www.GarrettPlanningNetwork.com.

Begin Your Journey: Open an Account with Your Financial Advisor

Once you have met with your advisor and have agreed to follow the outlined financial strategy, you open your new account and begin to fund it with your assets. You may write a check or you may transfer various assets into your new account. You may currently be holding the physical certificates of various investments in your lockbox, or you may be holding assets in one or more brokerage accounts that you want to consolidate. Whatever the case, you must determine the type of account that best suits your needs.

An asset management account. Almost all major investment firms offer some sort of asset management account that they recommend for accounts with assets over $5,000. These accounts offer some added "bells and whistles" that are ideal for people attempting to simplify their money management. These accounts hold a broad variety of investment alternatives such as stocks, bonds, mutual funds, annuities, and unit trusts. And they usually have some sort of interest-bearing checking or money market account associated with them. This feature allows fast access to your investment money should you need it while allowing your emergency money to draw a competitive rate of return.

Other services that may be included:

▶ A debit card
▶ Unlimited check-writing privileges
▶ Borrowing on margin
▶ Internet services
▶ Electronic bill payment services
▶ Summary statements of capital gains and loss

Dear Dad,

Thanks for the birthday money. You'll be pleased to know I've finally created a financial plan for myself, and I intend to put your gift to good use. I feel like I just woke up to the fact that I'm 25 years old, I have no financial assets, and I'm $5,500 in debt, with an interest rate of 12 percent. I met with a financial planner, and together we realized I can get out of debt by paying $259 for 24 months; then I can begin to save 10 percent of every paycheck until I turn 65. Retirement seems a long way off, but by saving a fixed amount of $3,600 for 35 years (assuming a 9 percent annual rate of return), I could expect to accumulate a nest egg of approximately $776,558.71.

I also realized I can save the extra $300 per month by keeping my current car and by taking my lunch to work four out of five days each week. I know you've been nudging me to do this since I graduated college, but I just couldn't focus on it until now. Thanks for being patient with me, and thanks again for your gift.

—Jim

Some of these may carry additional charges. In addition, most full-service firms charge an annual fee for an asset management account. You will want to check with your financial advisor to find out the costs.

At most full-service firms, you are still able to hold assets in a standard personal account. This type of account is different from the premier account just described, because it is designed with little or no frills. This type of account is used by newer investors who don't yet have the assets to qualify for the premier account or don't anticipate needing any additional services.

Evaluating the information you've gathered is also important. A skilled advisor may uncover pitfalls in your current financial plan that can be quickly corrected simply because they were identified. However, just as a medical doctor can run lab tests and has other equipment to evaluate certain types of information, it is the doctor's *advice and judgment* that you count on for a correct diagnosis and treatment. In the same way, many investors have found that although they may be able to gather the correct data, they don't have the expertise to go to the next step, and they need a professional's advice. Don't be afraid to ask for help: your money, your savings and investments, and your financial future are too important!

Getting Ready to Merge
Getting Married or Moving in Together

If *starting out* for you means starting out as a couple, either because you're getting married or moving in together, then all of the financial issues discussed in this book need to be addressed with this other person in mind. In this chapter we will focus on these issues primarily from the point of view of married couples, because the marriage contract introduces legal implications for your finances, but we will also address how these issues affect nontraditional couples.

Marriage will bring many changes in your financial situation that will affect your financial goals and objectives, personal property, assets, debts, retirement accounts, savings, taxes, and more. However, with proper planning and good communication, two people can combine their assets and live nearly as cheaply as one with a better quality of life and an increased standard of living than they could if they remain single.

Obviously, more financial planning will be necessary if or when you add children. Raising and educating children costs are estimated to be over $100,000, and you will need to budget to meet these needs. In addition, you must decide the kind of home and car you need, the type and amount of insurance that will adequately cover you and your possessions, and the estate planning techniques that are most appropriate for passing on your assets to your children. Because you're just starting out, this chapter will cover only the most critical issues that you might want to start thinking about at this time.

In most relationships, one person usually takes the lead in financial matters, though it doesn't matter which partner does. In any case it's important that the other partner play an active role in setting priorities and making financial decisions.

▶ Plan Your Itinerary! Talk about Your Finances

Small financial problems often grow into larger ones, simply because some couples find it difficult to talk about money. Financial problems are the #1 reason that couples argue and are the leading cause of divorce. Before marriage, many people avoid the subject, in the belief that their partners are fiscally fit, only to find out that they are deeply in debt or have other problems managing money.

Before and during your marriage or when you move in together, it's important to communicate openly about money on a regular basis and keep each other informed of your financial situations. As your financial discussions progress, you will get a good sense of each other's spending habits, and you will freely share your dreams for the future. Many couples set aside time each week or each month for a financial discussion and then reward themselves afterward with a dinner out or a movie.

Kick the Tires before Starting Out Together: Give Yourself a Financial Checkup

Begin your financial checkup by asking your partner to join you in filling out the budgeting worksheets from Chapter 1 and the saving and investing worksheets from Chapter 6 that you completed on your own.

1. Determine your joint net worth, which will give you a chance to add up all the assets and liabilities you have accumulated at this point in your relationship. Set financial goals as a couple. This task will test your ability to compromise, which is an important skill. To meet your financial goals, you must prioritize the things that are more and less important to both of you in the short-, medium-, and long-term future.
2. Complete a cash flow statement together, which will give you an accurate picture of both of your spending habits. Knowledge about your cash flow

will also update you on how much income you and your partner earn collectively.

3. Create a monthly household budget, which will help you put your priorities into practice as you allocate your income among competing spending priorities.

4. Assess your risk tolerance as a couple. This task will determine whether you and your partner agree on how much investment uncertainty you should accept to earn higher returns on your assets. In most relationships one partner is dedicated to capital preservation, whereas the other is more willing to take risks.

5. Develop a record keeping system: Make sure you both know where you keep all your important documents, which financial advisors you consult, and how to contact your relatives for help in an emergency.

Once you have completed these exercises, discuss what you have learned about your financial situation and your attitudes toward your personal finances. Don't expect to agree about everything all or even most of the time. Listen to your partner's point of view and take it into account when you decide on a final course of action.

Not only is making important financial decisions together good for the longevity of your relationship or marriage, this habit also allows both partners to understand their current financial affairs. It's not uncommon for a person who has taken care of the family finances alone for decades to die suddenly, leaving the spouse without a clue about their investments, insurance, estate plans, and every other financial matter. Unscrupulous insurance salespeople, brokers, and financial planners often try to capitalize on the spouse's naiveté. Confusion and lack of knowledge about the couple's financial situation may also cause the surviving partner to panic and make hasty decisions or be indecisive, when he or she needs to take action to protect the family's financial future. Because you're just starting out on your financial journey and your life together as a couple, we hope this situation won't happen to you. In any case you should be aware of this scenario because illness or an accident can strike at any time.

Prenuptial Agreements

If you're getting married, you might consider signing a prenuptial agreement. The subject generally raises a few eyebrows, and many people believe that signing one dooms a marriage. But a prenuptial agreement can be the right move when one partner has more assets or earns much more than the other, has substantial debt, has children from a prior marriage who need to be protected in case of death or a second divorce, owns part or all of a business, or is planning to go back to school. (The prenuptial agreement can help ensure that the working partner's contribution to the other partner's education is properly rewarded.) If any of these scenarios applies to you, you should consider discussing a prenuptial agreement with a lawyer, and then broach the idea to your partner. A domestic partnership agreement is the equivalent document for unmarried couples and is highly recommended.

Map Your Trip Together: Create a Budget for Both of You

Before you can make any financial decisions, you need to know the value of what you own, how much you owe, how much you bring in monthly after taxes, and where your money goes each month. Here's a quick overview of what you need to do before you can create a budget. Toward that goal, you need to

1. Collect all your financial documents (bank and credit card statements, checkbooks, information on assets and debts, employer benefit packages, and so on).
2. Put together a combined balance sheet of all of your assets and debts. Set aside money for an emergency fund with living expenses for three to six months.
3. Determine what you are spending your money on and try to spot areas where spending can be reduced.
4. Review your combined investment portfolios. Rebalance them if your combined portfolio is overweighted in any particular asset class.
5. Find ways to maximize contributions to your retirement funds.
6. Obtain a copy of your credit report to see if any issues will affect your future borrowing power.
7. Split up financial duties between the two of you, such as paying the bills, consolidating statements, and keeping tabs on your savings. Then assign responsibilities based on each person's strengths. Or you can assign duties to the partner who needs to develop a particular skill, and then have the other partner provide coaching. This last point is particularly important, so the next section provides further suggestions.

Who Pays the Tolls? Assigning Responsibility for Your Joint Finances

One partner should assume and maintain the role of "budget director." Many couples fall into their respective roles because they're good at it, like it, or have more time, or by default when one partner refuses. These roles often can be logical and efficient, provided that the budget director is good at managing money. Once this pattern is set, it can last for years unless some event causes the routine to change.

Both partners should be involved with the household finances in some way, even if this means trading off partial or full-time responsibility every six months, every year, or every other year. By getting involved with your household finances on a regular basis, you develop an awareness of your financial obligations, limitations, spending patterns, and overall current financial status. You also have a better appreciation of how expenses are going up.

This awareness is especially important for personal relationships. There may be times when the partner managing the finances must announce, "No, we can't afford that item or luxury right now." This news can easily conjure up a whole gamut of reactions for the uninvolved partner. Feelings of confusion and misunderstanding may lead the other partner to retort, "What do you mean? We were just paid three days ago. What are you doing with all the money?"

If the partner who blew up had firsthand experience with the bills and budget for the previous six months, it would be easy to see the reason for the decision to cut back. It's difficult to know what you can and cannot afford each month when you start losing a sense of what it costs to run your household. You may not be as in touch with how last-minute events or expenses gobble up the discretionary cash, how computer interests or other hobbies tend to get more expensive, and how household repairs manage to keep piling up.

As mentioned, this mutual awareness is especially important if the designated budget director is suddenly in an accident, or develops a long-term illness, or if the relationship ends. If the other partner is already familiar with the financial picture and the location of all the papers and records, then the trauma of the loss will not be compounded by the fear of taking on the new, often terrifying responsibility of handling all the finances.

Even without traumatic circumstances, many people find that carrying the responsibility of making all the financial decisions alone for many years becomes a major burden. Therefore, couples should work together or trade off the responsibility of paying the bills and keeping records. Decide what works best for your situation and then follow through on that decision.

Handling Bank Accounts

One of your first challenges as a couple will be how to manage the checking accounts. The most common options include combining all the accounts right away or keeping three separate checking accounts: yours, your partner's, and your joint account. Whatever the agreement, it is critical for each of you to have your own "fun" money to be used as each of you desires. If one partner wants to hit the golf course and the other wants to run by the manicurist, the fun money provides freedom and independence without guilt.

Employee Benefits

As discussed in Chapter 3, one of your greatest assets can be the employee benefits you earn as part of your compensation. Your health, term life and disability insurance, retirement savings plans, profit-sharing programs, college education loans, savings bond payroll deduction plans, and other benefits can provide a solid financial foundation that would be prohibitively expensive to duplicate on your own.

Therefore, you should coordinate your employee benefits with those of your partner. For instance, your spouse's company may offer an excellent health insurance policy but a limited retirement savings plan, whereas your firm may provide a mediocre health plan but a generous savings plan. In this case, use your partner's health policy as the primary insurer and deposit the maximum possible in your savings plan. Many companies offer cafeteria-style plans that allow you to mix and match benefits according to your needs. If both you and your partner have such flexibility, you may be able to create a combined set of benefits far superior to those you could obtain on your own.

Discuss your benefits package with your partner so that he or she understands the main provisions of the plans. The material explaining your company's benefits package may be dense and complex, but it is worth reading, at least to learn the basics of how your insurance and savings programs function. Understanding both your own and your partner's benefits packages also helps you plan in the event that one partner loses his or her job, and you both must rely on the remaining benefits.

In addition, there's good news for unmarried couples. More employers are offering domestic partner benefits to their unmarried employees. This generally includes health insurance and may include other benefits. However, the employer's contribution is taxable to the employee as additional income, whereas married employees pay no taxes on the benefits they receive.

Dealing with Taxes

Although some relief from the marriage penalty tax went into effect in 2003, a two-income couple with more than $120,000 of household income still owes more in taxes than two single people with the same total income. So prepare now to pay more to Uncle Sam come April 15.

If you're getting married, you'll have the choice of two filing statuses, married filing jointly or married filing separately. Discuss your situation with your tax and financial advisor to determine which situation works to your advantage. Usually married filing jointly is the better option.

The tax code offers married couples many advantages. For example, married couples filing jointly move into higher tax brackets at higher levels of income than single people. Most couples save money if they file a joint return. However, it could be more profitable to file separately if both partners earn significant taxable income and generate substantial deductions. The IRS says that you must file separately if you and your partner have different fiscal years in which you must report income, if one partner is a nonresident alien, or if either partner is claimed as a dependent on someone else's return.

The tax law establishes other rules for married couples as well. For example, if one partner does not work, the other can still contribute up to $4,000 in a spousal IRA, on top of $4,000 to a regular IRA.

Unmarried couples can maximize their deductions by arranging tax deductible expenses so that the higher wage earner pays for the tax deductible items and makes the charitable contributions, while the other claims the standard deduction. In addition, when opening a joint investment account, unmarried couples should consider whose Social Security number is listed as primary on the account. If all else is equal, use the Social Security number of the partner in the lower tax bracket. This person will report the income at the lower rate.

What's Your Ultimate Destination?
Identify and Prioritize Your Goals

After you've dealt with the basics of your short-term financial decisions, such as banking, it's time to consider your longer-term financial goals. It's important to identify and document your most important life goals before making major decisions, including buying a home, saving for when you have kids (if that's in your future), and retirement, though it's far away. So sit down together and ask yourselves, "What are our financial objectives?"

For example, suppose you're a young couple, and you both want to retire at age 66. You also want to send your children to private high schools, fund your children's college education, and take an annual family trip to Europe. Each of you should now ask yourself, "Would I have any additional goals if I knew I had only two years left to live?" Let's say that you would not change your goals, but your partner would like to spend less time at work and more time with the family. Though your partner makes a good living, you quickly realize that your resources might not fund everything you want to do. So you reconsider the goal that originally prompted your question, within the context of all your goals. In other words, it's not enough to identify your goals; you need to prioritize them, too.

If you're working with a financial advisor, he or she must first understand your goals and priorities before developing a worthwhile plan and offering meaningful advice. If you're developing a financial plan on your own, realize that goal setting is the first and most important step in the financial planning process. There's no advantage to implementing a plan or taking advice that leads you to goals that are not right for you. And, as noted, when two people are involved, you might not have the same goals! So you need to discuss what your goals are as a couple. Here are some simple methods to help you identify and prioritize your goals:

1. *List all your financial goals.* Sit down with a piece of paper or at a computer and start listing your goals as quickly as you think of them. Don't stop to evaluate them; just identify and list them. Afterwards, ask yourself what else you would want to do if you knew you had only two years to live and add those things to your list. This exercise isn't intended to be morbid; it's intended to help you see what's most important to you.

2. *Prioritize your goals.* If you could achieve only one goal, which would it be? Mark it as your number one goal. If you could achieve only two goals, what's the second goal you would choose? Mark that as your second goal, and continue the process until all the goals on your list are numbered. No two goals can have the same number.

Sometimes it helps to segregate your goals into two categories—critical and noncritical—and then prioritize them within each group. Still another technique is to group the items on your list by time frame; for example, one group of goals must be accomplished within the next two years, another group within five years, and so on.

Consider doing this exercise separately first, with each of you completing your own list of prioritized goals. Then meet to discuss what you have in common and your differences. Create a third list that represents your jointly agreed upon goals and priorities. With this level of careful thought and discussion, you can then go forward with your mutual plan as a couple and your coordinated individual plans.

The Road at the Edge of a Cliff: Handling Credit and Debt as a Couple

Now come the trickier issues: You and your partner may have different attitudes toward debt. It is amazing the trauma that results when couples don't communicate about their finances. It seems that with most couples, one is a spender and the other is a saver. One partner controls the finances, the other partner has no clue as to what the financial situation is. Or one may abhor the idea of borrowing money, whereas the other may have grown up in a family accustomed to charging even life's basic necessities. Discuss your attitudes about debt and come to an agreement about how much debt is appropriate for your income and lifestyle.

It's no wonder that money is one of the top three reasons for marital problems and divorces. If financial woes don't cause divorce, they will cause stress, anxiety, arguments, and communication problems. Secrets in a relationship regarding finances always manage to come out.

Keep in mind that although a couple's finances may be intertwined, each partner's credit records are maintained separately by credit reporting bureaus (as long as each partner has established credit in his or her own name). Therefore, it is important that both partners take out credit cards and other loans in their own names and repay these loans responsibly. Many people are shocked to discover that they cannot qualify for credit when a partner dies because they never established a credit history in their own names. Once you establish credit, devise a strategy to manage it wisely. Set a limit on the total amount of your income devoted to debt service. While you are young, this may be up to 20 percent; over time, reduce it to 10 percent or less. If you have several credit cards or lines of personal credit, it may make sense to consolidate them into one or two accounts that offer the lowest interest rates and annual fees.

If you bring significant debt, such as college loans, into your marriage or relationship, assume primary responsibility for paying off those loans. The faster you dispose of the debts, the better it is for your relationship.

When you consider taking out loans against the value of your assets, make such decisions jointly. This rule of thumb applies to home equity, margin, and life insurance loans, as well as to borrowing against your retirement plan assets at work. The more you share responsibility for credit decisions with your partner, the easier it will be for the surviving partner to carry on if the relationship doesn't last or when one of you dies.

But if you have joint credit cards (in both your names), keep in mind that if your relationship ends or you get divorced, you need to notify your creditors of the divorce and cancel your open joint credit cards. If you do not take care of this task, both of you will be liable for the debts. Creditors must be notified and must authorize any agreement that is drawn to release and remove the partner who will not be responsible for the payment.

Obstacles in the Road: Dealing with Credit Problems

Many people just starting out wonder what constitutes an "appropriate" amount of debt, so they can avoid having "too much debt." The best way to stay out of debt is to pay your credit cards bills in full at the end of each month. People lose control by not keeping track of what they are charging.

Here are some general guidelines. Most people can afford to pay 10 percent of their net income to installment debt, which is the name for the debt you carry from month to month on your credit cards not including their mortgage payments. If you pay out more than 15 percent to installment debt, you need to cut back. More than 20 percent being paid out to installment debt could result in financial problems. It is important to have a budget sheet that you fill out every month to make sure you are not paying out more than 10 percent of your income towards installment debt. If you are, make adjustments in the following month to reduce your debt.

It's worth repeating: It's important that both of you know exactly what is going on with your finances so that there are no surprises. Review your budget sheet together once a month and try to live within your income.

Many compulsive spenders often try to hide their credit card purchases and loans. If the spending gets so out of control that debts are too high and can't be paid, that's usually when the confession comes. The worse thing to do in a relationship is to keep secrets, especially when it comes to money. It is important for partners to keep each other informed on all financial matters. As noted previously, if your partner leaves or dies, and you're not aware of the condition of your finances beforehand, tremendous pressure and problems could result from this lack of communication. The bills are still due and payable, even if you or your partner is gone.

If you're married and living in a community property state, such as California, you need to know that both the husband and the wife are responsible for repayment of the debts. Credit cards and loans that are in a husband's name will affect only his credit rating. And only if the wife's name is listed on a debt can the credit card company report the payment history on her credit report.

One way to handle credit problems that affect you both is to write a plan for repayment that you and your partner can live with. Consolidating the credit card debt into one credit card may be an option. This plan would mean transferring balances from one credit card to another lower-interest credit card. If you own a home, you could consider taking out a consolidation loan to pay the credit card companies.

However you decide to repay your partner's debts, you should limit yourself to one credit card each. Pay cash whenever possible and pay the credit card balances off every month. If that isn't a possibility, pay as much as you can, not just the minimum due. Keeping outstanding balances low will lower the amount you'll pay in interest.

Special Caution Ahead: What Women Need to Know about Credit

Every woman, whether married or single, should have credit in her own name. Should anything ever happen to your partner, you may not be able to establish credit for yourself if the family credit is in your husband's name. Your credit report could show "no record found," which can be interpreted as having bad credit. This situation is more likely to occur if you are a homemaker who is suddenly widowed or divorced, and you have no job or income.

If your credit cards are only in your husband's name, you are considered only a user of the card. Sometimes the credit card company will reflect this status on your credit report, but don't count on it. Check your credit report from all three credit reporting agencies to see if any of the accounts you are using are listed on your credit report.

The Equal Credit Opportunity Act was designed to stop discrimination against women. You may not be denied credit because you are a woman or because you are married, single, widowed, divorced, or separated. As long as you show that you are creditworthy and fall into the guidelines of the credit application, you can't be discriminated against.

When you apply for credit, you don't have to use Miss, Mrs., or Ms. with your name. You can choose to use your married name, maiden name, or a combination of both surnames, such as Mary Williams Smith. If you apply for a credit card while you are married, you do not have to have your husband as a cosigner or be listed jointly if your income is high enough to meet the stated requirements.

Whether you are married or single, credit reporting agencies use your Social Security number as an identification source. If you apply for new credit under your married name, the Social Security number will be cross-referenced and reported with your maiden name. This situation could cause your credit report to be merged with your married and maiden names. All of your accounts would appear on one report. In any case if you've recently married, you should contact each of your creditors and give them your new married name (if you've changed your name) and other pertinent information. Have your creditors update their credit files and notify the credit reporting agencies of the changes. When creditors are notified of your name change and their files are updated, they will report your active accounts and any activity on your accounts to the credit reporting agencies using your new name.

If you later divorce and decide to use your maiden name, you should ask each of your creditors to change your name on their accounts at that time, too. Once the creditors' records are updated, it is important that they notify the credit reporting agencies. On the other hand, if at that time you have some negative accounts in your husband's name, don't have those changed into your name because that will hurt your own credit report. You want to try and build a credit report without any negative information.

Share the Driving: Your Credit Can Rebuild Your Partner's Credit

On the other hand, one partner's credit can often help rebuild the other partner's credit. For example, suppose you had a major financial crisis in the past and couldn't pay your bills, which was reported on your credit report. If your partner has credit cards in his or her name and has good credit, your partner can add you to that account, which will help you rebuild your credit. Your partner will be adding you as a joint applicant. The credit card company will then request your Social Security number and income information.

Because your partner is the primary applicant, your partner is ultimately responsible for all payments. If they are made on time, this fact will be picked up by the credit reporting agency and reflected as a positive entry. The more positive entries on your partner's credit report, the easier it will be for you to reestablish your own credit.

Nevertheless, it's still advisable for you to have a credit card solely in your name. You never know when you might need it for an emergency.

▶ The Road to Home Ownership

As discussed in Chapter 4, the decision to rent or buy a place to live is a major one. It's even more complex for couples, although you have the benefit of joint assets and incomes to help you afford it! Even so, buying a home or renting an apartment is a major financial commitment. It plants your roots in a particular community and leads you to adopt a certain lifestyle. Therefore, you and your partner must agree on the kind of housing you want, where you want it, and how much of your income you will devote to it.

First, assess your short- and long-term housing needs. If you have no children now but expect to within a few years, consider getting a home large enough to accommodate them, if you can afford it. If you do not plan to have children, you'll look for different amenities in the home of your dreams than a couple with children. For example, you won't need a playroom, but you might want an elegant dining room.

If you and your partner agree to purchase a home and assemble enough money for a down payment, you must then shop for a mortgage. You can qualify for a much larger loan if you and your partner earn two incomes rather than one. Most people advise that you assume the mortgage jointly, and therefore own the home, at least at first. Later when you are more concerned with estate planning, you might transfer the property into the name of only one partner to make maximum use of the $1,500,000 (currently) exemption from estate taxes.

On the other hand, some people feel that owning property jointly is one of the biggest errors you can make, at least from the perspective of protecting yourself from a lawsuit. The simple act of dividing up property between you and your partner can be the difference between losing half of what you own and all of what you own.

Most married couples purchase real estate jointly. They do so because the bank or their real estate agent told them that it should be that way. Here's the danger: Suppose one of you is a teacher and the other is a doctor. A teacher has a fairly low-risk occupation as far as lawsuits go, but the doctor has a very high-risk occupation. If the doctor is sued, a creditor might be able to force the sale of the family home, because the doctor's name is on the title. In that scenario, it would be better for the teacher to own the property solely (subject to community property rules and whether or not the lender would require both names).

In some states, real estate held jointly by husband and wife cannot be attached by a creditor of one partner (known as *tenancy by the entirety*). The only option that a couple has in this situation is to wait it out until the creditor gives up or the debtor partner dies. If both husband and wife are young, the judgment will create a problem if they want to sell or refinance the property. Furthermore, the protection is lost if the couple is divorced and may not continue if one partner files for bankruptcy protection.

Finally, in states where there is *community property* (California, Louisiana, Texas, Wisconsin, Idaho, Arizona, Nevada, New Mexico, and Washington), all property of a husband and wife acquired after their marriage is presumed to belong to both partners, regardless of how it is titled. Thus, a creditor can usually attack all of the marital property, even if only one partner is liable for the debt. It may be desirable to convert community property in writing to "separate" property, and then divide up the property between the partners according to their risk of being sued. In the event of a lawsuit, the couple can prove which property is the separate property of the non-debtor partner.

Before you apply for a mortgage, discuss with your partner the pros and cons of a fixed-rate versus a variable-rate mortgage. (Refer back to Chapter 4 for details.) The fixed-rate loan costs much more on a monthly basis, at least in the first few years, but it provides you with the security that your interest rate will never rise. On the other hand, the variable-rate loan saves money up front, but it exposes you to the risk of higher interest rates in the future. You and your partner should weigh the financial advantages of the variable-rate loan against the emotional security of the fixed-rate loan until you agree on which mortgage is right for you as a couple.

The emotional aspect of buying a home can be extremely intense. Conventional wisdom has it that women view their homes as nests, men as their castles and investments. Whether or not this is true, when buying a home with a spouse or partner, it's wise to talk about the kinds of compromises that may be in order. This type of discussion will create less room for conflict when the time comes to choose. Roadmap 7.1 can help you establish your own priorities. It lists the factors that are essential in buying a home, those on which you will compromise if necessary, and those that don't matter at all. And although these decisions may not seem like financial issues, they will most certainly affect the cost of the home you buy, so you should consider them before you go out to look at any real estate. Similarly, use Roadmap 7.2 to fill out the profile of your needs and wants, and to consider the housing factors common in the area in which you want to buy. Both of these variables will be affected by what you can afford.

Sharing the Driving: Forms of Joint Ownership

When you buy a home with someone else, the wording of the deed determines each person's respective shares of ownership, legal rights, and the disposition of the property on the death of one of the buyers. Depending on state law, there are three types of joint ownership:

1. *Tenancy in common.* In this case each owner has the right to leave his or her share to chosen heirs.
2. *Joint tenancy with right of survivorship.* The surviving owner automatically becomes complete owner.
3. *Tenancy by the entirety.* This type of joint ownership is a special form of joint tenancy for married couples.

If the owners have unequal shares, tenancy in common is the usual form. Except in the case of tenancy by the entirety, any owner has the right to force a division or sale of the property (partition). When there is more than one owner, it is important to check with an attorney or the title company to make sure that the deed clearly states the desired form of ownership.

Paying the Tolls: Securing a Mortgage

Before you can worry about how to take title of a home of your own, you need to get a mortgage (unless you can afford to buy a home with an all-cash payment, which few people can do). The good news is that even if one of you

Roadmap 7.1

House Hunting: What Matters Most to You?

Before you start house hunting, consider which factors are most important to you. Rate on a scale of 1 (unimportant) to 10 (very important):

Proximity to work	___	Storage space	___
Quality and proximity of schools	___	Room for hobby	___
Condition/age of house	___	Room for entertaining	___
Type and age of roof	___	Home office	___
Fireplace(s)	___	Ease of maintenance	___
Landscaping, view	___	Mature trees	___
Garage requirements	___	Light and sunshine	___
Number of bedrooms	___	Sidewalks	___
Number of baths	___	Lot size and usability	___
Pool or spa	___	Expandability	___
Computer wiring	___	Security system	___
Large kitchen	___	Breakfast nook	___
Deck, patio	___	Formal entry	___
Separate dining room	___	Workshop	___
Family room/great room	___	Formal living room	___
Community pool	___	Neighborhood park	___
Gate guarded	___	Ample guest parking	___
Active adult (over 55)	___	Tot lot	___
Neighborhood rules (CC&Rs*)	___	Other	___

*Covenants, conditions, & restrictions

Roadmap 7.2

Your Personal Home Owning Profile

After you've analyzed the ratings in Roadmap 7.1, establish your own priorities: the home factors that are essential, those on which you will compromise if necessary, and those that don't matter at all.

Absolute Musts	Nice to Have	Don't Matter
_____	_____	_____
_____	_____	_____
_____	_____	_____
_____	_____	_____
_____	_____	_____

has poor credit, you can probably still get a mortgage. Married individuals can secure mortgages in their own names provided they meet the required income, assets, and creditworthiness guidelines. Federal law prohibits discrimination based on marital status; therefore, one partner's adverse credit cannot be used to deny a loan to the other partner.

But you need to be careful when you are applying for new credit, whether it is for a credit card or a mortgage. If you have poor credit, your credit as a couple will not be strong enough to qualify even if your spouse has excellent credit. This fact is especially true if your income is higher than your spouse's.

A credit grantor will look at the wage earner who is making the highest salary to determine an approval or denial. If your income is higher than your spouse's, the credit grantor will evaluate the application on your creditworthiness rather than your spouse's.

The best thing to do in this case is to have your spouse apply for new credit. Once that has been approved, your spouse can request another credit card for you with your name on it. This can be either a joint or a user card.

Your spouse will be responsible for making the payments, and this positive outcome will help you add new credit to your credit report.

If you are applying for a mortgage, wait until the new credit is seasoned for at least a year. Your spouse should then apply for a mortgage as an individual. If the mortgage is approved, your spouse will be the one solely responsible for the payments, and your spouse's name will be the one recorded on the title. After the loan is closed, your spouse can file a *quit claim deed*, adding your name to the title, which must be recorded with the county recorder's office. However, a quit claim deed might invalidate the mortgage and/or title insurance. Then, after you have reestablished your credit history, you can refinance your home jointly.

You also need to make sure that you're not carrying too much debt. Some people find that when they prequalify for a loan, their debt ratios are too high for the lender to approve a mortgage for a home in the price range they're looking for. This situation occurs sometimes even if both incomes are good and the credit history is excellent. When you are being qualified for a mortgage, the lender wants to make sure that you can afford to make the payments. The lender will add up all your debts and the new proposed house payment, including the principal, interest, taxes, and insurance (PITI). Sometimes a homeowners association fee (see Chapter 4) is added as well. The lender will not count installment loans that you are currently paying off if there are 10 months or less left on the loan.

The lender will then divide this total by your gross monthly income. This amount will give the lender a ratio for qualification. Each loan program demands different qualification ratios. If yours is too high, ask your lender how high the ratio can be. Determine what debts you must pay off to get to the right ratio. You may need to consider purchasing a less expensive house to meet the demands of the qualifying ratios that are required.

▶ Planning for a Long Journey: Investing Together

One of the most difficult habits for couples to establish is regular investment. The easiest way to begin such a program is with the defined contribution or salary reduction retirement plan offered by your employers. Enroll as soon as you are eligible and deposit as much money out of your paycheck as possible. Not only do these plans allow you to amass a sizable, tax deferred retirement fund, but they also cut your current tax bill because you contribute pretax dollars.

In addition, deposit a certain amount of your earnings in a joint savings and investment account aside from the one your employer offers. Start by building your emergency cash reserve until it is equivalent to at least three months' (preferably six months') salary. You never know when you might need this money to cover unexpected medical bills, travel, or the breakdowns of major appliances. (For more information on cash instruments, see Chapter 6.)

In the years when you are childless, strive to save at *least* 10 to 20 percent of your gross income. While you are young, invest most of the money in growth-oriented vehicles, such as growth stocks or aggressive growth and international stock mutual funds. You can also enroll in one of the approximately 1,000 dividend reinvestment plans (DRIPs) described in Chapter 6 on stocks. Or you can set up an automatic investment program with almost any mutual fund. The fund debits your bank account for the amount that you specify, whether it is $50 or $5,000, on a biweekly, monthly, or quarterly basis.

By accumulating a substantial pool of capital when you have fewer financial obligations, you will be better able to afford the expenses of raising and educating your children when they arrive. Unfortunately, many couples believe that they have little reason to save until they have children, so they spend lavishly in their childless years. But, as shown in Chapter 6, the beauty of compound interest means that your young years are the best time to invest, not the best time to spend wildly.

Once you have children, financing their education often becomes a top priority as an investment goal. The earlier you start saving money and the more appropriately you invest it, the greater the chance that you will be able to pay for college without extreme financial strain. Some funds require as little as a $100 minimum initial investment when you establish an automatic investment plan of at least $50 per month or $250, with subsequent investments of $20.

If you wait until your children become teenagers, you will have to come up with much more money, and you probably will not be able to cover college expenses. This outcome may mean that you and your children will assume thousands of dollars in college debt.

If you do not plan to have children, concentrate on building your retirement fund. Invest more aggressively in your younger years; then become more conservative as you move toward retirement. It's important to set up a disciplined investment program so you do not spend your excess cash frivolously.

▶ Preparing for a Long Journey Together

If you've made a commitment to your partner to spend the rest of your lives together, then even though you're just starting out, you need to start thinking and preparing for how you'll protect and finance your journey. There are several aspects to this commitment: insurance, retirement planning, and estate planning, including creating a will with designated beneficiaries. The next sections describe each of these topics in more detail.

Insuring Your Journey

Married couples need all five types of insurance—auto, disability, health, homeowners/renters, and life—whether they have children or not. However, the amount of coverage often depends on the existence of children. Here's a quick overview of these five types.

Auto Insurance. Your auto insurance contract depends mostly on the kind of car you own. Make sure you have adequate, comprehensive liability protection to defend your family's assets against a lawsuit. Retain enough collision coverage to pay for the complete repair of your car in case of an accident. For unmarried couples, if an auto insurance company will not issue joint coverage, the owner can be listed as the primary driver and the partner as an occasional driver on the policy (but if this is the case, the partner must only drive "occasionally").

Disability Insurance. This type of insurance is critical to protect your partner and family against a major loss of income if you get injured or ill *while not* on the job. Your employer may offer some disability coverage, but if not, look into buying a supplemental policy that would generate between 60 and 70 percent of your salary if you cannot work. If both partners work, each should have adequate disability protection. Under some circumstances, Social Security will also pay disability benefits.

Health insurance. This insurance protects your family against the high costs of medical care. If you receive health insurance through your employer, you probably have to pay part of the premium for family coverage, but it is far less expensive to buy insurance in this manner than on your own.

If your employer offers the option, look into *health maintenance organizations* (HMOs) or *preferred provider organizations* (PPOs) in your area. These plans should emphasize preventive care and employ a knowledgeable staff of pediatric generalists and specialists if you have children.

If your company does not offer health insurance, see whether you can join an HMO, a PPO, or another managed care plan during an open enrollment period. If you can't, you may have to opt for extremely expensive family rates by signing up with Blue Cross/Blue Shield during their open enrollment period.

If your company offers flexible spending accounts (FSAs) for health and dependent care, take advantage of them. (Refer back to Chapter 3 for more about these benefits.)

Homeowners insurance. This protection guards you against liability claims and the loss or damage to your possessions if you own a home or an apartment. When you marry, you merge possessions from two households, giving you more objects to insure. Children require a whole new roster of items, from bassinets and cribs when they are infants to computers and electronic gadgetry when they are teenagers. Keep your homeowners policy up to date as you purchase valuable new items.

Unmarried couples living together have additional concerns. If an adult lives in a residence, and this person's name is not on the deed, he or she may not be covered by the homeowners policy. They need to be added to the homeowners policy, if possible, or get renter's insurance.

Life insurance. This type of insurance protects your partner and your children from the negative financial consequences of your unexpected death and the resulting loss of income. If your partner also produces income and you need that income, you need insurance policies for both of you. When you add children to the equation, your need for life insurance grows even more. If your partner stays home to care for the children, insurance coverage helps the surviving partner pay for day care and other essential domestic services.

Once you determine the optimal amount of coverage, decide whether to buy *term insurance* or a form of *cash value insurance,* such as whole life, variable life, or universal life. If you are young and earn a limited income, term coverage is less expensive but pays only if you die. As you get older, you might convert some of that term insurance into a cash value policy that allows you to build a tax-deferred savings reserve.

Insurance experts argue the merits of both term and cash value policies. Term insurance is certainly cheaper, and if you systematically invest the difference between the term premium and the cash value premium, you will probably come out ahead with the term. However, if you are not a disciplined saver, you might find that the cash value policy provides a form of forced savings, which might come in handy when you retire. If you accumulate a considerable amount of cash value and no longer need the death benefit, you can convert the savings into an annuity that will pay you monthly income for the rest of your life.

Comprehensive disability and medical insurance is more important than ever for people who may not have a biological family they can depend on for support. Long-term care insurance is important for unmarried couples, too, because Medicaid prohibits the healthy partner from living in the jointly owned home, unless they buy out the interest of the ill partner who requires Medicaid.

▶ Next Exit: Retirement

If you and your partner are in good health, you probably will live well into your eighties, nineties, or beyond. Start saving as early as possible to fund these decades when you will earn no salaries. If both you and your partner are offered a defined contribution plan through your employers, enroll and have as much deducted from your paychecks as allowed. At a minimum, contribute the most that your employers will match in cash or stock, and then increase it with each pay increase.

In addition to contributing to employer-sponsored savings programs, build your regular joint savings and investment portfolios as much as possible. Set aside a certain amount—no less than 10 to 20 percent—of your incomes, and invest for long-term growth.

Although you can still count on Social Security to provide some income at retirement, don't expect it to cover a significant portion of your living expenses. Many experts strongly encourage younger people not to count on receiving Social Security survivor benefits. The combination of your company-sponsored retirement plans, personal investments, and Social Security will be needed to provide your income for many years of leisure.

Appendix B lists resources that will give you more information on how to estimate your expenses in retirement, how much money you might expect to accumulate by the time you retire, and how much you'll need to save to meet your retirement goals.

The End of the Road: Estate Planning and Creating Your Wills

When you get married, you will want to change the beneficiaries on your 401(k)s, IRAs, and life insurance. You will also need a will so that your assets are disbursed properly when you die. A will is critical when minors are involved so you can name their guardians! If either of you has children from a previous marriage, a will is especially important to ensure that they receive a stake in your estate.

Married couples should plan their estates whether or not they have children. If a couple has no will, many state laws say that all the assets of one partner automatically transfer to the surviving partner when the first one dies. A few states have different laws of intestate succession that prevent this transfer from being automatic. Under federal estate law there is an unlimited marital deduction, so no estate taxes are due when assets pass from one partner to the other. However, the estate of the surviving partner may be taxed heavily when he or she dies if none of the assets has been gifted away or no estate planning has been done.

If you have children, one of several kinds of trusts may be appropriate. You also need a will to designate a guardian to raise your underage children if both you and your partner die unexpectedly. If you have no children, make provisions to pass your assets to whomever you please, whether it be your next of kin, a close friend, or your favorite charity.

Issues for Unmarried Couples. For unmarried couples (same-sex and heterosexual couples), revocable trusts can be extremely effective tools for estate planning. For estate tax purposes, you own the assets individually, though the trust document specifies what happens to the trust property when you die, thus avoiding probate delays and related costs.

One potentially huge landmine for unmarried couples is the inadvertent gifting between unmarried partners. Married couples are allowed unlimited marital transfers, but unmarried people are not. When an unmarried couple wishes to transfer a large asset like a home from individual to joint owner-ship to avoid the gift tax, one strategy is to draft a document that spells out the terms of a gradual ownership transfer. To do this, consult an attorney experienced in estate planning or real estate transactions.

Finally, unmarried couples must take responsibility for many estate planning issues that married couples take for granted. Here are some other issues to consider.

1. *Create a Living Will.* This document stipulates the kind of medical care you wish or do not wish to receive if you become incapacitated due to illness or injury.

2. *Establish a Durable Power of Attorney for Health Care.* This document gives your partner visitation rights, the power to make health care deci-sions, and the authority to hire and fire medical personnel. Your partner can even limit which next of kin may visit.

3. *Establish a Durable Power of Attorney for Finances.* This document allows you to name someone to manage your financial affairs if you are unable to do so. Without this document, you would have to ask a court for the authority to take over the financial affairs of an incapacitated partner.

4. *Establish a Domestic Partnership Agreement.* This document is impor-tant to the implementation of your estate and financial plans. It's wise to consider the possibility that the relationship may end. A Domestic Partnership Agreement will ensure that you are as prepared as you can be for any foreseeable outcome.

5. *Consider Signing Parenting Documents.* A paternity statement is a writ-ten acknowledgment of fatherhood. A parenting agreement is a written commitment stating the desire to parent together. It includes language that states the intention to continue co-parenting, even if the relation-ship ends.

6. *Funeral Arrangements.* Create a document that expresses each of your wishes concerning your after-death plans. If no document exists, the next of kin has the right to make the funeral arrangements.

For more information on issues facing unmarried couples, see Appendix B for some useful Web sites.

Appendix A

An Itinerary

Here's a quick review of what to do as you set out on the road to getting started in life.

Stop #1. Take stock of your present financial situation: You can't make any changes until you know what you have.

- ▶ Create a budget: List all of your current assets, debts, regular monthly bills, and everyday expenses, so you know how much money you really have and where it's going.
- ▶ Create yearly and monthly budget worksheets to help you plan how you'll spend your money to help you keep track of your expenses. Careful budgeting is also a good way to make sure you'll have enough.
- ▶ List all your financial goals: short-term, medium-term, and long-range, so you will know how you want to spend and save your money.

Stop #2. Arrange for more money to be available to you: Obtain a line of credit, but use it wisely.

- ▶ Establish good credit for yourself. Find out all you can about how credit cards work. Then determine what your credit cards charge for late fees, interest rates, and other penalties if you don't pay in full on time.
- ▶ Find out how your credit history is created, and how you can get a copy of your credit report.
- ▶ Learn how to manage debt, so you don't fall too far behind in your credit payments.

Stop #3. Get the most out of your employer: Don't pull just your salary but maximize all your company benefits.

- ▶ Make sure you understand the details of your company's retirement plan, and how you can optimize your participation by contributing the maximum savings allowable.

▶ Ask if your employer offers a tuition reimbursement plan and consider if it could benefit you in advancing your career.

▶ Understand the ins and outs of your company's health, life, and disability insurance plans and find out if your company offers a Flexible Spending Account. Then learn how to set aside pretax dollars to pay for these expenses.

Stop #4. Improve your living situation: Explore whether you can afford a better apartment or buy your own home (without breaking the budget).

▶ Decide how much you can afford to spend on housing and determine whether you should rent or buy a home.

▶ Consider sharing your living situation and its expenses with a roommate, but make sure you know what you're getting into legally, financially, and with respect to lifestyle.

▶ Calculate whether you can afford to buy a home. If so, decide how expensive a home you could own and the type of housing you'd prefer: traditional single-family house, condo, co-op, or townhome.

▶ Find out how to get prequalified for a mortgage. Then start budgeting and saving for a down payment and the monthly mortgage payments.

▶ Learn all you can about various types of mortgages and how to obtain the one that's right for your personal financial situation.

Stop #5. Get the best car for your money.

▶ Determine what you need in terms of a car's features and options, and figure out what you will need your car for.

▶ Consider buying a used car instead of a new car, and find out how to do so without getting burned.

▶ Determine whether it is better to buy or lease a car, and find out how to get a car loan.

Stop #6. Start saving as soon as you can! The beauty of compound interest is most helpful the sooner you start saving:

▶ Discover how much your money can grow during your lifetime if you start saving now.

▶ Review your financial goals and start setting aside the money you'll need to realize them.

► Assess your risk tolerance so you'll know the type of investments you'll be most comfortable with. Are you a conservative or aggressive investor?

► Learn the basics of investing and find out what your options are. Decide how much you want to invest in cash, bonds, and stocks.

► Assess how well your investments are performing. Compare your portfolio with the right benchmarks so you can make intelligent, unemotional investing decisions.

► Consider hiring a professional financial planner, and find out all you need to know about different types of planners, the services they offer, and how they're compensated.

Stop #7. If you're getting married or moving in with your partner, keep in mind that financial decisions affecting both of you should be made jointly:

► Talk openly about all aspects of your finances: your assets, debts, spending habits, saving habits, approach to investing, and financial goals. Failure to communicate about these factors is the number one reason couples split up, so find out how to avoid being part of this statistic!

► Create a household budget that you can both live with.

► Assign one person to manage the day-to-day finances, pay the bills, and make sure you're on the right track toward achieving your financial goals. This isn't a job that can be shared easily.

► Make sure you understand how your individual credit and debt history affects you as a couple, and work together to improve and manage credit and debt.

► If you decide to buy a home, discuss candidly what each of you wants and what you can jointly afford, and learn what you need to know about joint ownership and securing a mortgage.

► Take advantage of your employee benefits collectively: One of your employers may offer better plans that both of you can use.

► Make sure you have the necessary insurance (life, car, disability, health, and homeowners/renters) so that both of you are protected.

► Discuss your retirement plans, and create the appropriate estate planning documents in this process. The end of your journey may be decades away, but you'll be happier and more at ease if you get started now.

Bon voyage!

Appendix B

The Best of *Starting Out*: A Resource Guide

▶ Bibliography

The following books were used as resources for this book. In addition, we have provided lists of other books and Web sites that offer more detailed information on some of the topics covered in this book. We hope you will find all of these resources useful.

Cook, Frank. *You're Not Buying That House, Are You? Everything You May Forget to Do, Ask, or Think about before Signing on the Dotted Line.* Chicago: Dearborn Trade Publishing, 2004.

Garrett, Sheryl. *Just Give Me the Answers: Expert Advisors Address Your Most Pressing Financial Questions.* Chicago: Dearborn Trade Publishing, 2004.

Goodman, Jordan E. *Everyone's Money Book,* 3rd ed. Chicago: Dearborn Trade Publishing, 2001.

Irwin, Robert. *Buy Your First Home!* 2nd ed. Chicago: Dearborn Trade Publishing, 2000.

Lank, Edith. *The HomeBuyer's Kit,* 5th ed. With Dena Amoruso. Chicago: Dearborn Trade Publishing, 2001.

Lawrence, Judy. *The Budget Kit: The Common Cents Money Management Workbook,* 4th ed. Chicago: Dearborn Trade Publishing, 2004.

Lewis, Allyson. *The Million Dollar Car and $250,000 Pizza: How Every Dollar You Save Builds Your Financial Future.* Chicago: Dearborn Trade Publishing, 2000.

McNaughton, Deborah. *All about Credit: Questions (and Answers) about the Most Common Credit Problems.* Chicago: Dearborn Trade Publishing, 1999.

Sacks, Ed. *The Savvy Renter's Kit.* Chicago: Dearborn Trade Publishing, 1998.

Smith, Steven B. *Money for Life: Budgeting Success and Financial Fitness in Just 12 Weeks!* Chicago: Dearborn Trade Publishing, 2004.

Steinmetz, Thomas C. *The Mortgage Kit,* 5th ed. Chicago: Dearborn Trade Publishing, 2002.

Weiss, Mark. *Condos, Co-Ops, and Townhomes: A Complete Guide to Finding, Buying, Maintaining, and Enjoying Your New Home.* Chicago: Dearborn Trade Publishing, 2003.

▶ Recommended Books and Web Sites

Chapter 3: Win the Race: Getting the Most out of Your Employer

Beam, Burton, Jr. and John McFadden. *Employee Benefits,* 6th ed. Chicago: Dearborn Trade Publishing, 2001. Address: 30 S. Wacker Dr., Chicago, IL 60606. Telephone: 1-312-836-4400; 1-800-245-2665 (http://www.dearborn trade.com). A comprehensive explanation of employee benefits, updated to incorporate the Health Insurance Portability and Accountability Act and the implications of the latest tax laws.

Downing, Neil. *Maximize Your Benefits: A Guide for All Employees.* Chicago: Dearborn Trade Publishing. To order, see contact information above. The author translates tax, legal, and investment jargon into simple terms and explains how company benefits fit into a household's overall financial plan. He also discusses issues related to pensions, vesting, and defined benefit plans and health plans.

Ferraro, Genevieve, Sheryl Lilke, and R. Newkirk. *Solutions Handbook: For Personal Financial Planning, Business Planning, Employee Benefits, Estate Planning.* Chicago: Dearborn Trade Publishing.

Fundamentals of Employee Benefits Programs, 5th ed. Washington, DC: Employee Benefit Research Institute, 1996. Contact information: Employee Benefit Research Institute, 2121 K St., N.W., Suite 600, Washington, DC 20037-1896. Telephone: 1-202-659-0670 (http://www.ebri.org). A comprehensive overview of all major employee benefits programs, including Social Security, pension plans, salary reduction plans, profit-sharing plans, employee stock ownership plans, SEPs, IRAs, health insurance, dental insurance, drug prescription plans, group life insurance, disability insurance, education assistance, FSAs, MSAs, and temporary leave programs.

Neuman, R.E. *The Complete Handbook of U.S. Government Benefits.* Encinitas, CA: United Research Publishing, 2003. This guide gives you information about Social Security, business loans, educational benefits, grants, pensions, and home and farm loans.

Chapter 4: Moving on Down the Road: Renting an Apartment vs. Buying a House

Irwin, Robert. *Buying a Home on the Internet.* New York: McGraw-Hill, 1999.

_____. *Tips and Traps When Mortgage Hunting.* 2nd ed. New York: McGraw-Hill, 1998.

Chapter 5: Travel in Style: Buying A Car

Bragg, W. James. *Car Buyer's and Leaser's Negotiating Bible,* 3rd. ed. New York: Random House, 2004. Order Dept., 400 Hahn Rd., Westminster, MD 21157. Telephone: 1-800-733-3000 (http://www.randomhouse.com). This manual shows readers how to negotiate with confidence, establish the right price for any new vehicle, find the actual dealer cost, determine the true wholesale value of your trade-in, and negotiate by phone or fax without going to the showroom.

The Complete Car Cost Guide, 2004. Campbell, CA: Intellichoice, 2004. Annual editions. To order: Intellichoice, Inc., 471 Division St., Campbell, CA 95008-6922. Telephone: 1-408-866-1400 (http://www.intellichoice.com). A wealth of information on the cost of owning any of the nearly 400 cars analyzed. Includes dealer cost, suggested retail price, and projected annual costs for five years, including tax, licensing, insurance, depreciation, maintenance, and repairs. Many informative charts.

The Complete Small Truck Cost Guide. Annual editions. Campbell, Calif: Intellichoice. Intellichoice, 471 Division St., Campbell, CA 95008. Telephone: 1-408-866-1400 (http://www.intellichoice.com). A wealth of information on the cost of owning any of the many trucks analyzed in the book. Dealer cost, suggested retail price, and projected annual costs for five years, including taxes, license, insurance, depreciation, maintenance, and repairs, are included. Many informative charts.

Consumer Reports New Car Buying Guide. Des Moines, IA: Consumer Reports Books. Annual editions. Address: Consumer Reports Books, P.O. Box 10637, Des Moines, IA 50336. Telephone: 1-800-500-9760 (http://www.consumerreports.org). Complete new car pricing information for 2004.

Consumer Reports Used Car Buying Guide. Consumer Reports Books, P.O. Box 10637, Des Moines, IA 50336. Annual editions. Telephone: 1-800-500-9760; http://www.consumerreports.org). Complete used car pricing information for the year 2004.

Edmunds New Cars & Trucks Buyer's Guide, 2005. Los Angeles: Edmunds.com, 2005. Annual editions. To order: Edmunds.com, P.O. Box 25906, Los Angeles, CA 90025 (http://www.edmunds.com). New car prices for the year 2005.

Edmunds Used Cars & Trucks Buyer's Guide. Los Angeles: Edmunds.com, 2005. Annual editions. To order: Edmunds.com, P.O. Box 25906, Los Angeles, CA 90025 (http://www.edmunds.com). Used car and truck prices for the year 2005.

Gillis, Jack, ed. et al. *The Luxury Car Book.* New York: HarperResource, 2004. Address: Harper Resource, P.O. Box 588, Dunmore, PA 18512. Telephone. 1-212-207-7000; 1-800-331-3761 (http://www.harpercollins.com). Features full-page entries on a wide range of new and late-model new and used luxury cars.

_____. *The Ultimate Car Book.* New York: HarperResource, 2000. To order: Harper Resource, P.O. Box 588, Dunmore, PA 18512. Telephone: 1-212-207-7000; 1-800-331-3761 (http://www.harpercollins.com). Includes reviews, ratings (value, fuel economy, insurance costs, complaints, crash tests, maintenance), safety features, and advice on warranties, lemon laws, reducing insurance costs, and other car owner issues.

Lieb, Jeremy. *Buying a Car on the Internet.* New York: McGraw-Hill Trade, 1999. To order: McGraw-Hill Trade, P.O. Box 543, Blacklick, OH 43004. Telephone: 1-800-634-3961 (http://www.mcgraw-hill.com). Shows how to take advantage of online resources and find the right car with all the information needed to take control of the sale negotiations.

Nader, Ralph and Clarence Ditlow. *The Lemon Book: Auto Rights.* Wakefield, RI: Moyer Bell Ltd., 1990. To order: Moyer Bell Ltd., Kymbolde Way, Wakefield, RI 02879. Telephone: 1-401-789-0074 (http://www.moyerbell.

com). Offers advice on how to avoid scams by car dealers and what to do
if you end up with a lemon.

National Automobile Dealers Association. *N.A.D.A. Official Used Car Guide.*
Published quarterly. To order: NADA, 8400 Westpark Dr., McLean, VA
22102. Telephone: 1-800-248-6232. (http://www.nadaguides.com).

Nerad, Jack R. *The Complete Idiot's Guide to Buying or Leasing a Car.* New
York: Alpha Books, 1999. (an imprint of Penguin Group USA. Easy-to-
read information on car buying.

Raisglad, Ron. *Buying and Leasing Cars on the Internet.* Los Angeles: Renaissance Books, 1998. To order: Renaissance Books, 5858 Wilshire Blvd.,
Suite 200, Los Angeles, CA 90036. Telephone: 1-800-452-5589 (http://
www.renaissancebks.com). Step-by-step instructions on how to use the
Internet to conduct every type of automotive transaction: buying, selling,
leasing, financing, getting insurance, and even repairs.

Sclar, Deanna. *Buying a Car for Dummies.* Foster City, CA: IDG Books, 1998.
To order: IDG Books, 919 E. Hillsdale Blvd., Suite 400, Foster City, CA
94404. Telephone: 1-650-653-7000; 1-800-434-3422 (http://www.idg.com)
(http://www.dummies.com). Offers useful information to help the reader
buy a car, using questions, checklists, and worksheets that are all organized for easy access.

Stubblefield, Mike and John Harold Haynes. *The Haynes Used Car Buying
Guide: The Haynes Manual for Evaluating and Buying a Used Car.* South
Bound Brook, NJ: Motorbooks International, 1996. To order: Motorbooks
International, D&S Hobbies, 34 Main St., South Bound Brook, NJ 08880.
Telephone: 1-732-271-0800 (http://www.onerrave.com). Describes the
kinds of things to look for when buying a used car that you wouldn't
know unless you are knowledgeable abour cars.

Car Buyer and Car Pricing Services

▶ American Automobile Association. Address: 1000 AAA Dr., Heathrow,
FL 32746-5063. Telephone: 1-407-444-7000 (http://www.aaa.com). A fed-
eration of motor clubs throughout the United States and Canada. Offers
information about cars and travel. AAA provides emergency road service and towing, emergency check acceptance, travel agency services,
tour books, Triptiks to help you find the most efficient way to get where
you're going, hotel discounts, accident insurance, TripAssist (a 24-hour
emergency hotline for legal, medical, or travel-related problems), trav-

eler's checks, discounts on car rentals, auto repair referral service, AAA credit cards, and the *AAA New Car and Truck Buying Guide*, which provides performance and specification details for most new cars. AAA also performs research and provides driver education to improve automotive safety.

▶ *AutoAdvisor.com*. This Web site (http://www.autoadvisor.com) offers services to locate the new or used car you want and helps you to research the lowest price and to negotiate the sale or lease of a car. All of these services carry a price tag.

▶ CarBargains. This is the Web site (http://www.carbargains.com) for the consumer magazine *Checkbook*. For a fee, this site will solicit bids from up to five local dealers in your area for the car that you want. You take the lowest bid and purchase the car from the dealer.

▶ CarSource. 700 Larkspur Landing, Suite 199, Larkspur, CA 94939. Telephone: 1-415-927-2886; 1-800-517-2277 (http://www.carQ.com). This national car buyer's service will help you find the model you want for the best possible price and terms. CarSource will also refer you to a car buying service in your state, if that service is a certified member of the National Association of Buyer's Agents (NABA). The Association requires that their members work for fees from consumers only and receive no compensation from car dealers.

▶ Consumer Reports Auto Price Service. 101 Truman Ave. Yonkers, NY 10703. Telephone: 1-800-203-5454 (http://www.consumerreports.org). This car pricing service provides a computer printout comparing the sticker price to the dealer's invoice for the makes and models you choose. The printout tells you exactly what the dealer paid for the car and every option, and also informs you of factory-to-customer and factory-to-dealer incentive programs. Consumer Reports also offers a Used-Car Price Service (1-800-258-1169) that provides the current market value price of any car you describe in your region. Trade-in, buying, and selling prices of used cars are based on the car's age, mileage, options, and condition.

▶ *Money.com*. This *Money* magazine general personal finance Web site (www.money.cnn.com) offers an auto link that helps you find a new or used car for the price you want to pay. The site includes information about safety, economy, and maintenance, and has links to http://kbb.com and http://carsmart.com, where you can browse new car prices and purchase a car online.

▶ Nationwide Auto Brokers. 29623 Northwestern Hwy., Southfield, MI 48034. Telephone: 1-248-354-3400; 1-800-521-7257 (http://www.nationwide-auto. com). This national car broker will send you an invoice and sheet listing a car's options. If you use the service to buy a car, they will refund the cost of the option sheet and tell you the suggested markup and vehicle cost.

Chapter 7: Get Ready to Merge: Getting Married or Moving in Together

Resources for Unmarried Couples

Berkery, Peter. JK Lasser's Gay Finances in a Straight World.

_____. *Personal Financial Planning for Gays & Lesbians.*

4 Steps to Financial Security for Lesbian & Gay Couples, by Harold Lustig (Ballantine Books, an imprint of Random House Publication Group)

Nolo Law for All (http://www.nolo.com)

Lambda Legal (http://www.lambdalegal.org)

Alternatives to Marriage Project (http://www.atmp.org)

Garrett, Sheryl and Neiman, Debra, *Money Without Matrimony: The Unmarried Couple's Guide to Financial Security* (Dearborn Trade, 2005). http://www.moneywithoutmatrimony.com

Hayden, Ruth, *For Richer, Not Poorer: The Money Book for Couples* (HCI, 1999).

Index

Notes

Notes

Notes

Notes